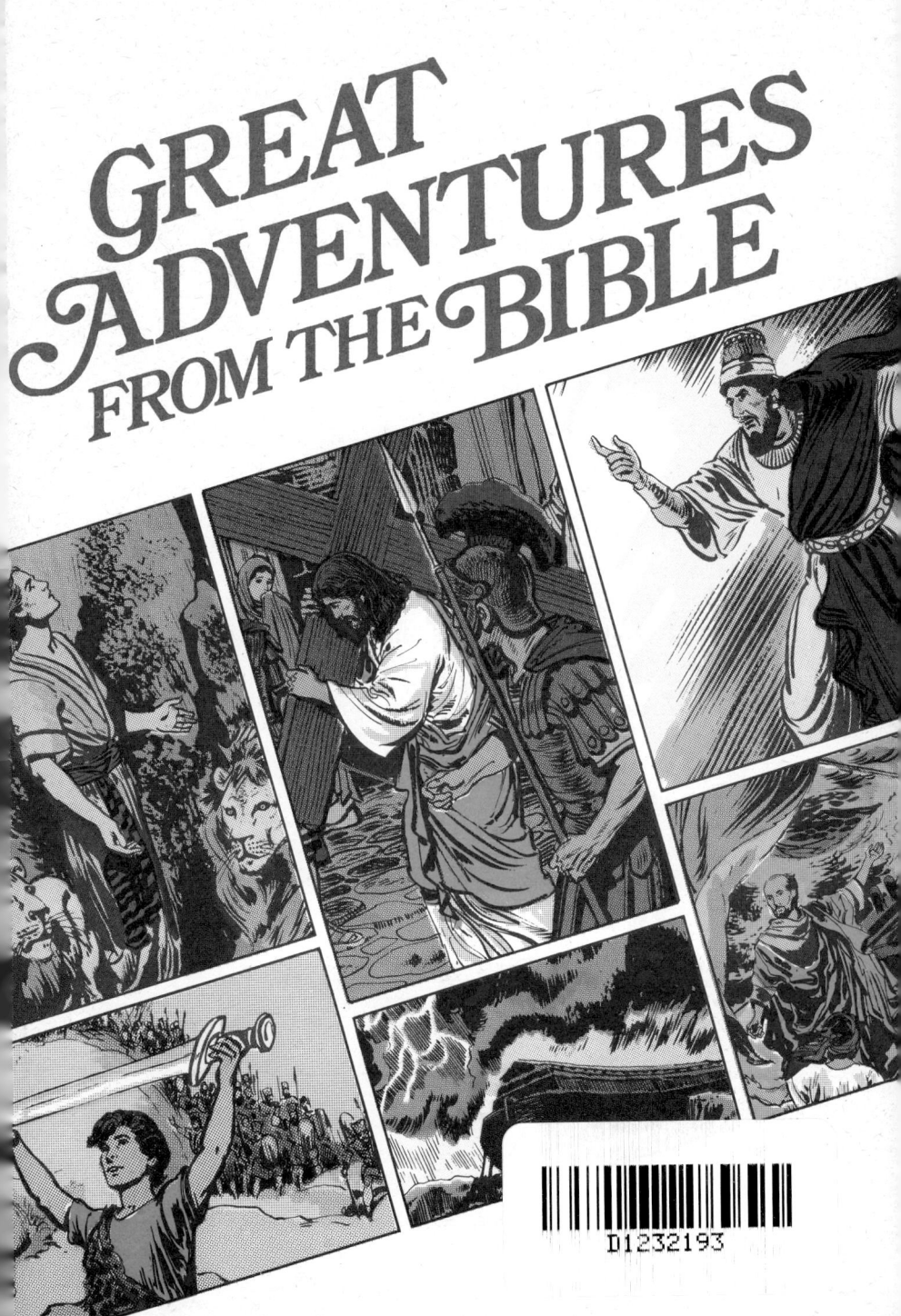

GREAT ADVENTURES FROM THE BIBLE

Chariot Books is an imprint of the David C. Cook Publishing Co.
David C. Cook Publishing Co., Elgin, Illinois 60120
David C. Cook Publishing Co., Weston, Ontario

GREAT ADVENTURES FROM THE BIBLE
© 1984 by David C. Cook Publishing Co.

Cover and division pages designed by Wayne Hanna/HANNA & HANNA

The adventures found in this book are excerpted from the **Picture Bible** © 1978 by David C. Cook Publishing Co. See page 224 for more information

Printed in the United States of America
First Printing, 1984
90 89 88 87 86   5 4 3 2

LC: 84-70184

Library of Congress Cataloging in Publication Data

Great adventures from the Bible.

   Illustrated by André Le Blanc.
   Summary: A collection of Bible stories presented in a comic strip format.
   1. Bible stories, English—Comic books, strips, etc.
[1. Bible stories—Cartoons and comics. 2. Cartoons and comics] I. Le Blanc, André,
1921-   , ill.
BS550.2.G69 1984   220.9'505   84-3246
ISBN 0-89191-848-5

CONTENTS

Temptation in the Garden

God created the world and all the plants and animals in it in six days. He took the man and woman he had created to the garden of Eden and showed them the beauty and fruitfulness of it. God said to Adam and Eve, "You are free to eat from any tree in the garden; but you must not eat from the tree of the knowledge of good and evil, for when you eat of it you shall surely die."

BUT ADAM AND EVE KNOW THEY HAVE DISOBEYED GOD. THEN THEY HEAR HIS VOICE CALLING THEM.

I'M AFRAID!

QUICK—LET'S HIDE!

IN THE STILLNESS OF THE GARDEN THEY HEAR GOD ASK: "HAVE YOU EATEN THE FRUIT THAT I TOLD YOU NOT TO EAT?"

EVE GAVE ME SOME FRUIT—AND I ATE IT.

THE SERPENT TEMPTED ME!

"BECAUSE YOU DISOBEYED ME," GOD SAID, "YOU MUST LEAVE THIS BEAUTIFUL GARDEN AND WORK FOR YOUR LIVING."

LOOK! A FLAMING SWORD GUARDS THE ENTRANCE— WE CAN NEVER GO BACK.

WHERE CAN WE GO? WHAT CAN WE DO?

Adam and Eve are banished from the garden forever.

8

Jealous Brothers

OUTSIDE THE GARDEN OF EDEN THE LAND IS BARREN, HOT AND DRY. WEARY, ALONE AND FRIGHTENED, ADAM AND EVE SEARCH UNTIL THEY FIND A PLACE TO MAKE A HOME.

REMEMBER HOW BEAUTIFUL EDEN WAS? IF ONLY...

YES, IF ONLY WE HAD OBEYED GOD. WE MUST MAKE CERTAIN THAT WE TEACH OUR CHILDREN SO THAT THEY DON'T MAKE THE MISTAKE WE DID!

SO ADAM TEACHES THEIR SONS, CAIN AND ABEL, ABOUT GOD.

HE MADE THE EARTH AND EVERYTHING WE HAVE.

I LIKE TO THINK OF GOD GIVING ME MY LITTLE LAMB.

11

12

He looks around... and then he hears the voice of God asking: *"Where is Abel, your brother?"*

Terrified, Cain hears God's verdict—as punishment for murdering Abel, Cain must leave home and forever be a fugitive.

I—I don't know. Am I my brother's keeper?

GOD KNOWS I HAVE KILLED ABEL!

OH, GOD! PLEASE! THIS PUNISHMENT IS MORE THAN I CAN TAKE!

BUT GOD'S SENTENCE WAS CARRIED OUT. CAIN FLED TO A LAND CALLED NOD. THERE HE MARRIED AND BUILT THE FIRST CITY, WHICH HE NAMED FOR HIS SON, ENOCH.

ADAM AND EVE ARE HEARTBROKEN BY THE LOSS OF THEIR TWO SONS.

OUR HOUSE IS SO EMPTY AND STILL. OH, ADAM, WILL WE ALWAYS BE ALONE LIKE THIS?

WE BROUGHT THIS TRAGEDY ON OURSELVES, EVE—AND SO DID CAIN. BUT GOD HAS BEEN GOOD TO US. LET'S ASK HIM TO HELP US NOW...

IN TIME, A THIRD SON IS BORN TO THEM.

WE'LL CALL HIM SETH.

AND WE'LL TEACH HIM TO OBEY GOD THE WAY ABEL DID.

AGAIN ADAM AND EVE'S PRAYERS ARE ANSWERED, FOR SETH LEARNS TO OBEY GOD. TWO OF HIS DESCENDANTS ARE ENOCH WHO "WALKED WITH GOD AND METHUSELAH WHO DIED AT THE AGE OF 969—THE OLDEST MAN WHO EVER LIVED.

14

The
Giant Flood

YOUR WICKEDNESS CANNOT CONTINUE! TURN AWAY FROM YOUR IDOL WORSHIP! RETURN TO GOD WHO CREATED US AND GAVE US ALL THAT WE HAVE!

LISTEN TO NOAH! HE THINKS HE'S BETTER THAN ANYONE ELSE!

WHAT'S HIS GOODNESS DONE FOR HIM?

BUT NOAH REMAINS TRUE TO GOD. AND ONE DAY GOD SPEAKS TO HIM: "THE EARTH IS FILLED WITH VIOLENCE...I WILL DESTROY MAN WHOM I HAVE CREATED. MAKE THEE AN ARK, FOR BEHOLD I WILL BRING A FLOOD OF WATERS UPON THE EARTH."

NOAH OBEYS—AND SETS TO WORK BUILDING AN ARK ACCORDING TO THE DIRECTIONS GIVEN HIM BY GOD.

POOR NOAH, HE THINKS HE CAN FLOAT A BOAT ON DRY LAND.

WHAT WILL HE THINK OF NEXT?

WHEN THE ARK IS COMPLETED, GOD DIRECTS
NOAH AND HIS FAMILY TO ENTER... AND TO
TAKE WITH THEM SEVEN PAIRS OF EACH
KIND OF ANIMAL AND BIRD THAT IS GOOD
TO EAT, AND ONE PAIR OF EACH KIND NOT
USED FOR FOOD.

THE RAINS POUR DOWN STEADILY FOR FORTY DAYS AND FORTY NIGHTS.

WATER FLOWS OVER THE LAND AND RISES ABOVE THE MOUNTAIN-TOPS. ALL THE EARTH IS COVERED... ONLY NOAH'S GREAT ARK SURVIVES. THE FLOOD DESTROYS ALL THAT IS EVIL.

AT LAST THE WATER LEVEL DROPS AND THE ARK RESTS ON THE TOP OF THE MOUNTAINS OF ARARAT.

I WILL SEND OUT A DOVE; IF IT DOES NOT COME BACK WE WILL KNOW IT HAS FOUND LAND.

BUT THE DOVE RETURNS!

NOAH SENDS OUT A DOVE AGAIN, AND IT RETURNS.

AN OLIVE BRANCH! THAT MEANS SOME LAND MUST BE DRY AGAIN.

SEVEN DAYS LATER, NOAH SENDS OUT A DOVE A THIRD TIME. IT DOES NOT RETURN BECAUSE IT HAS FOUND A PLACE TO NEST.

SO, A LITTLE OVER A YEAR AFTER THE FLOOD BEGAN, NOAH STEPS ON DRY LAND ONCE MORE. HE, HIS FAMILY AND THE ANIMALS IN THE ARK ARE THE ONLY CREATURES ON EARTH.

HOW GOOD IT IS TO WALK ON THE GROUND AGAIN!

YES—TO FEEL GRASS UNDER YOUR FEET AND WARM SUNSHINE ON YOUR FACE.

ALL THAT WAS EVIL HAS BEEN DESTROYED. THROUGH US, GOD IS GIVING MANKIND A NEW START. WE MUST OBEY GOD—AND TEACH ALL WHO FOLLOW US TO DO SO.

AS SOON AS NOAH LEAVES THE ARK, HE BUILDS AN ALTAR. HERE HE THANKS GOD FOR HIS CARE AND ASKS GOD'S GUIDANCE IN HELPING NOAH AND HIS FAMILY TO MAKE A NEW START. THEN GOD MAKES A PROMISE TO NOAH AND TO ALL HIS CHILDREN, FOREVER...

Journey
in the
Unknown

In the years after the Flood, Noah's sons and their families move down to the river valleys. Some people move down the Euphrates River—and there build the city of Ur. The Bible traces the generations from Noah's son Shem to a tribal chieftain named Terah, who lives outside of Ur.

ONE DAY IN TERAH'S CAMP THERE IS GREAT EXCITEMENT—EVERYONE IS GETTING READY FOR A TRIP TO UR.

MAY WE TRADE OUR WOOL FOR ANYTHING WE WANT, FATHER?

YES, ABRAHAM. BUT FIRST YOU MUST HELP ME LOAD OUR SUPPLIES.

LOOK! GREEN BEANS AND MELONS!

WE'LL TRADE SOME OF OUR SUPPLIES FOR FRESH VEGETABLES. THEN YOU, HARAN AND NAHOR MAY GO INTO THE CITY.

A THROW STICK FOR YOUR BAG OF WOOL.

IT'S A DEAL!

IMAGINE THROWING A STICK THAT WILL COME BACK TO YOU.

WHAT IS THAT TOWER?

IT IS A TEMPLE TO THE MOON-GOD.

BACK HOME, ABRAHAM THINKS OFTEN ABOUT HIS VISIT TO UR. AND AS HE GROWS OLDER HE WONDERS ABOUT THE TEMPLE OF THE MOON-GOD.

ONE EVENING ABRAHAM TALKS TO SARAH, THE MOST BEAUTIFUL GIRL IN HIS FATHER'S CAMP.

IT'S ONLY THE MOON, SARAH, NOT SOMETHING TO WORSHIP.

ABRAHAM—BE CAREFUL. MANY PEOPLE HERE WORSHIP THE MOON-GOD. THEY MIGHT HEAR YOU AND DO YOU HARM.

WOULD YOU CARE, SARAH?

YES, ABRAHAM. EVERYONE EXPECTS YOU TO BE HEAD OF OUR TRIBE, SOMEDAY.

SARAH, I LOVE YOU AND WANT YOU TO BE MY WIFE. BUT IT'S ONLY FAIR THAT YOU SHOULD KNOW I DO NOT BELIEVE IN THE MOON-GOD. THERE IS ONLY ONE GOD—THE GOD WHO MADE THE MOON, THE STARS, THE SUN— EVEN US!

I LOVE YOU, ABRAHAM. BUT GIVE ME TIME TO THINK...

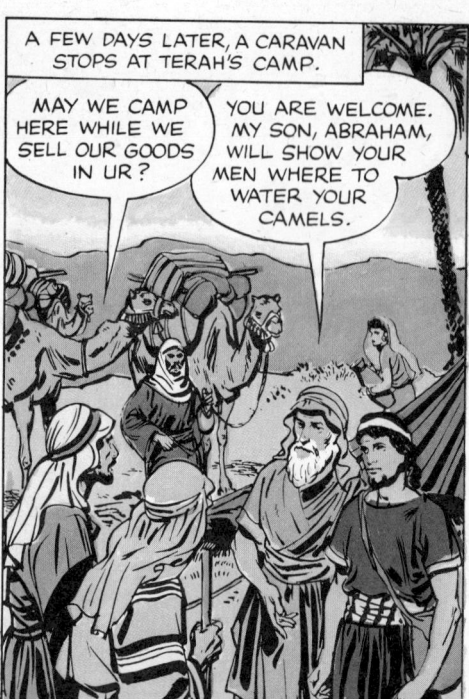

A FEW DAYS LATER, A CARAVAN STOPS AT TERAH'S CAMP.

MAY WE CAMP HERE WHILE WE SELL OUR GOODS IN UR?

YOU ARE WELCOME. MY SON, ABRAHAM, WILL SHOW YOUR MEN WHERE TO WATER YOUR CAMELS.

SO YOU COME FROM CANAAN. DO THE PEOPLE THERE WORSHIP THE MOON-GOD, UR?

NO, THEY HAVE THEIR OWN GODS, CALLED BAALS.

BAAL! THE MOON-GOD! EVERY-ONE HAS A DIFFERENT GOD. ABRAHAM, I BELIEVE AS YOU DO—THERE IS ONLY ONE GOD.

DO YOU, SARAH? THEN WE'LL BOTH TRUST IN GOD—NO MATTER WHAT HAPPENS.

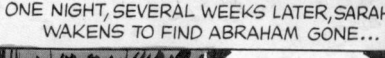

IT IS A FESTIVE DAY FOR ALL OF THE TRIBE WHEN ABRAHAM AND SARAH ARE MARRIED. DURING THE CEREMONY SARAH PRAYS TO GOD, ASKING FOR COURAGE TO STAND BY HER HUSBAND—FOR THEY ARE TWO AGAINST MANY WHO BELIEVE IN OTHER GODS.

ONE NIGHT, SEVERAL WEEKS LATER, SARAH WAKENS TO FIND ABRAHAM GONE...

ABRAHAM! ABRAHAM!

OH, ABRAHAM! ARE YOU ALL RIGHT? I WAS FRIGHTENED WHEN I FOUND YOU GONE.

SARAH, TONIGHT FATHER TERAH TOLD US WE ARE LEAVING UR AND MOVING NORTH. GOD PROMISED TO MAKE A GREAT NATION OF MY PEOPLE IF I WILL FOLLOW HIM. MAYBE THIS IS THE WAY I CAN LEAD OUR PEOPLE FROM THE WORSHIP OF FALSE GODS.

STRANGE...AT ONE TIME I WOULD HAVE BEEN AFRAID TO LEAVE UR. BUT NOW I'M EAGER TO GO.

NEXT MORNING—EARLY—TERAH DIRECTS THE WORK OF BREAKING CAMP...

LOT, NOW THAT YOUR FATHER IS DEAD, YOU WILL TAKE HIS PLACE AS HEAD OF YOUR FAMILY. WORK WITH YOUR UNCLES, ABRAHAM AND NAHOR.

AT LAST THE GREAT DAY ARRIVES. THE FLOCKS... DONKEYS LADEN WITH SUPPLIES...THE FAMILIES...ALL FORM A GREAT CARAVAN THAT PUSHES NORTH ALONG THE EUPHRATES RIVER.

I WONDER WHAT LIES AHEAD, ABRAHAM.

HAVE NO FEAR, SARAH, GOD WILL GUIDE US.

MAP OF TERAH'S JOURNEY.

AFTER A FEW DAYS OUT ABRAHAM CALLS A MEETING OF NAHOR AND LOT.

IT WILL BE COOLER FOR THE FLOCKS IF WE REST BY DAY AND TRAVEL AT NIGHT.

BUT WHAT ABOUT WILD ANIMALS?

WE'LL HAVE TO BE ON CONSTANT GUARD, NAHOR.

I AGREE WITH UNCLE ABRAHAM.

BUT ONE NIGHT A CARELESS GUARD LETS THE FLOCKS SCATTER...AND HUNGRY JACKALS ATTACK.

TOO MANY JACKALS—WE CAN'T STOP THEM!

WE CAN—AND WE WILL! PRAY FOR COURAGE AND STRENGTH!

IT WAS MY FAULT, ABRAHAM. WE WOULD HAVE LOST THE FLOCK IF YOU HADN'T CHASED THE JACKALS AWAY.

GOD GAVE ME THE COURAGE.

GOD? WHICH GOD, ABRAHAM?

THERE IS ONLY ONE GOD—GOD WHO MADE ALL THE THINGS THAT PEOPLE WORSHIP— THE MOON, SUN...

I WONDER IF NAHOR KNOWS WHAT ABRAHAM IS TEACHING!

31

NAHOR—YOUR BROTHER, ABRAHAM, IS TEACHING PEOPLE TO WORSHIP ONE GOD. HE SAYS THIS GOD MADE EVERYTHING. OUR GODS WILL BE ANGRY!

TELL NO ONE— WHEN THE TIME IS RIPE I'LL SPEAK TO MY FATHER.

AFTER MONTHS OF TRAVEL...

FRIEND, HOW FAR IS IT TO HARAN?

CROSS THE RIVER AT THE NEXT FORD— TWO DAYS' JOURNEY FROM THERE YOU WILL FIND THE CITY.

OUTSIDE HARAN, TERAH STOPS THE CARAVAN. HE AND HIS TWO SONS ENTER THE CITY.

MAY WE CAMP NEAR YOUR CITY?

STAY AS LONG AS YOU LIKE. OF COURSE—OUR MERCHANTS WILL BE GLAD TO SUPPLY YOUR NEEDS...

I'LL PAY 700 PIECES OF SILVER FOR YOUR CAMELS.

SOLD. HERE, SCRIBE, FIX UP A BILL OF SALE!

ABRAHAM WEIGHS OUT THE SILVER. SOON HE IS RAISING HIS OWN HERDS AND FLOCKS.

ALL GOES WELL IN TERAH'S CAMP UNTIL ONE DAY WORD SPREADS THROUGHOUT THE TENTS—TERAH IS ILL!

THIS IS THE TIME TO TELL YOUR FATHER ABOUT ABRAHAM'S GOD —BEFORE ABRAHAM BECOMES CHIEF!

NO, MY FATHER IS TOO ILL.

THAT NIGHT TERAH, THE OLD CHIEFTAIN, DIES. GRIEF-STRICKEN, HIS SONS LEAVE THE TENT OF THEIR FATHER...

OH, ABRAHAM!

AFTER THE PERIOD OF MOURNING...

WHAT ARE YOUR PLANS FOR THE TRIBE, ABRAHAM?

NAHOR, GOD HAS CALLED ME TO TAKE MY FAMILY—LOT'S, TOO, IF HE WISHES, AND LEAVE HARAN.

LEAVE? WHERE ARE YOU GOING?

I DON'T KNOW EXACTLY—BUT GOD PROMISED TO SHOW ME AND I HAVE FAITH THAT HE WILL LEAD ME.

A FEW DAYS LATER ABRAHAM'S AND LOT'S FAMILIES PULL OUT.

I TELL YOU ABRAHAM IS CRAZY. GOING SOMEPLACE...BUT HE DOESN'T KNOW WHERE!

MILE AFTER MILE ABRAHAM'S GREAT CARAVAN TRAVELS ON—STOPPING AT WATER HOLES TO REST AND WATER THE FLOCKS.

I KEEP WONDERING— WHAT IF WE'RE ATTACKED, OR THE PASTURES DRY UP, OR...

WE'RE NOT COWARDS, MAN! THERE ARE DANGERS, SURE, BUT ABRAHAM, OUR LEADER, HAS FAITH IN GOD. I'M LEARNING TO HAVE FAITH, TOO!

AT LAST THE CARAVAN REACHES CANAAN. THE PEOPLE THERE ARE FRIENDLY...

SO THE WEARY TRAVELERS MAKE CAMP ON A HIGH HILL. ABRAHAM BUILDS AN ALTAR AND GIVES THANKS TO GOD.

35

WHEN THE WEATHER GROWS HOT, THE HERDSMEN TAKE THE SHEEP INTO THE COOL VALLEYS.

A LION! HELP!

THE SAVAGE LION ATTACKS—BUT ABRAHAM'S MEN FIGHT BRAVELY.

WE'VE GOT HIM. TAKE CARE OF THE SHEEP!

THE HUNGRY LIONS RETURN DAY AFTER DAY. FINALLY LOT GOES TO ABRAHAM.

THE PASTURES ARE DRY AND WILD ANIMALS ARE ATTACKING THE SHEEP. WHAT CAN WE DO?

WE'LL MOVE SOUTH TO EGYPT UNTIL THE DRY SPELL IS OVER.

SO ONCE AGAIN THE TENTS ARE TAKEN DOWN, CLOTHING PACKED AND THE ANIMALS ROUNDED UP FOR THE MOVE SOUTH.

ABRAHAM, YOU ARE WORRIED. IS SOMETHING WRONG?

YES, SARAH, I'M AFRAID YOU ARE SO BEAUTIFUL THAT SOME MAN IN EGYPT MAY KILL ME SO HE CAN MARRY YOU. WHEN WE REACH EGYPT WE MUST NOT LET THE PEOPLE KNOW YOU ARE MY WIFE.

KILL YOU! OH, ABRAHAM, I'LL DO ANYTHING YOU ASK!

IN EGYPT WHILE ABRAHAM AND LOT INQUIRE ABOUT PASTURE LAND...

WHAT A BEAUTIFUL WOMAN!

WHO ARE YOU?

I'M ABRAHAM'S SISTER.

TAKE HER TO PHARAOH —HE WILL REWARD YOU FOR BRINGING SUCH A BEAUTIFUL WOMAN TO HIS COURT.

PHARAOH'S COURT! WILL I NEVER SEE ABRAHAM AGAIN?

IN THE EGYPTIAN PALACE, SARAH IS INTRODUCED AS ABRAHAM'S SISTER. PHARAOH IS AMAZED BY HER BEAUTY.

GIVE HER BROTHER, ABRAHAM, GIFTS OF SHEEP, OXEN, CAMELS AND SERVANTS. TRULY, HIS SISTER IS A BEAUTIFUL WOMAN!

OH, ABRAHAM, IF I DID NOT LOVE YOU SO MUCH I COULD NOT LIVE THIS LIE!

BUT SARAH'S PRESENCE IN PHARAOH'S COURT BRINGS TROUBLE. A PLAGUE BREAKS OUT...

THIS SICKNESS CAME UPON US AT THE TIME THE FOREIGN WOMAN WAS BROUGHT HERE. I HAVE LEARNED SHE IS REALLY ABRAHAM'S WIFE—NOT HIS SISTER. GET RID OF HER!

WHEN PHARAOH LEARNS TH TRUTH ABOUT SARAH, HE CALLS FOR HIS SOLDIERS.

BRING ABRAHAM AND SARAH TO ME—NOW!

WHEN ABRAHAM HEARS OF THE QUARRELS, HE TALKS OVER HIS NEXT MOVE WITH SARAH—

THIS TIME, SARAH, I'LL MEET THE PROBLEM AS I THINK GOD WOULD WANT ME TO.

THEN YOUR PLAN CANNOT FAIL.

THE NEXT DAY...

COME WITH ME, LOT. WE MUST DECIDE WHAT TO DO WITH OUR FLOCKS.

WHY SHOULD WE CLIMB A HILL TO DO IT?

THERE MUST BE NO MORE QUARRELING AMONG OUR PEOPLE. WE WILL SEPARATE— CHOOSE WHERE YOU WOULD LIKE TO GO AND I WILL TAKE WHAT IS LEFT.

I'LL TAKE THE VALLEY—NEAR THE CITY OF SODOM!

Abraham and his family had finally come to the land God had given to them.

The Stranger's Prophecy

any years pass. Abraham's flocks prosper and Lot's family grows. But all is not happy. Abraham and Sarah want children but so far they have had none. One night God speaks to Abraham in a dream.

"LOOK TOWARD HEAVEN, AND COUNT THE STARS, IF THOU BE ABLE TO NUMBER THEM:...SO SHALL THE NUMBER OF THY DESCENDANTS BE."

LATER, WHEN SARAH COMES TO HIM WITH A PLAN, HE LISTENS...

BY THE CUSTOM OF OUR PEOPLE I CAN GIVE YOU HAGAR, MY HANDMAID, AS A WIFE THAT SHE MIGHT HAVE A SON FOR ME.

GOD HAS PROMISED ME AN HEIR—PERHAPS THIS IS RIGHT...

HAGAR HAS A SON, AND HE IS THE PRIDE OF ABRAHAM'S HEART.

MY ISHMAEL IS A PROUD AND DARING ONE!

REMEMBER, HAGAR, HE IS MY SON! I ADOPTED HIM!

AS ISHMAEL GROWS TO BOYHOOD, HE IS THE CENTER OF ATTENTION THROUGHOUT THE CAMP...

...AND THE SOURCE OF TROUBLE BETWEEN HAGAR AND SARAH.

SOME DAY MY SON WILL RULE THIS WHOLE TRIBE!

HAGAR GETS MORE SURE OF HERSELF EVERY DAY!

ABRAHAM WORRIES ABOUT THE TROUBLE IN HIS CAMP. ONE DAY WHILE HE IS RESTING AT NOON TIME AND THINKING ABOUT ISHMAEL, HAGAR AND SARAH, HE LOOKS UP...

THREE STRANGERS APPROACH HIS CAMP. ABRAHAM GREETS THEM AND INVITES THEM TO REST AND EAT WITH HIM.

WHILE THEY ARE EATING, ONE OF THE STRANGERS GIVES ABRAHAM SURPRISING NEWS!

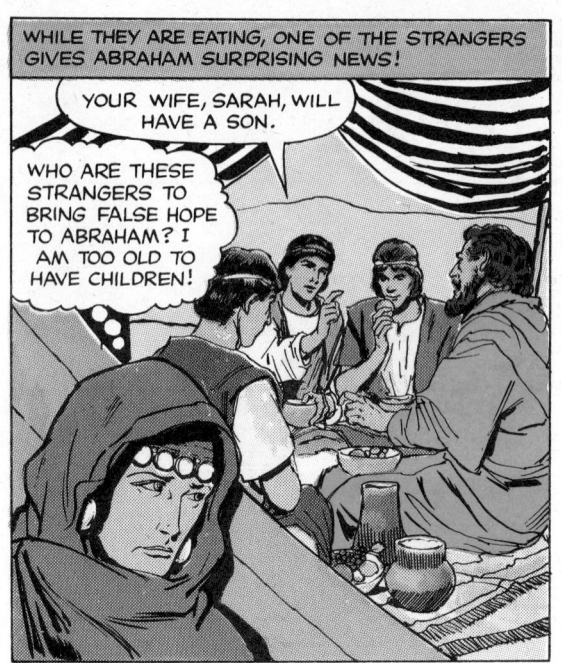

YOUR WIFE, SARAH, WILL HAVE A SON.

WHO ARE THESE STRANGERS TO BRING FALSE HOPE TO ABRAHAM? I AM TOO OLD TO HAVE CHILDREN!

BUT SARAH IS NOT THE ONLY ONE WHO OVERHEARS THE NEWS. HAGAR ALSO LISTENS AND IS AFRAID...

IF SARAH HAS A SON, WHAT WILL HAPPEN TO ISHMAEL —AND ME!

WHEN THE STRANGERS LEAVE, ABRAHAM WALKS A WAY WITH THEM.

THAT CITY OF SODOM IS SO WICKED THAT GOD MAY HAVE TO DESTROY IT.

THIS IS A MESSENGER FROM GOD! THEY ARE TALKING ABOUT THE PLACE LOT LIVES!

ABRAHAM PRAYS FOR SODOM, AND GOD PROMISES THAT THE CITY WILL BE SAVED IF THERE ARE TEN GOOD MEN IN IT.

MEANTIME TWO OF THE STRANGERS HAVE REACHED SODOM. ABRAHAM'S NEPHEW, LOT, WELCOMES THEM.

YOU ARE STRANGERS HERE. COME, STAY AT MY HOME.

THERE'S SOMETHING STRANGE ABOUT THOSE TWO MEN.

YES. LOOK—THEY'RE GOING TO LOT'S HOUSE. LET'S FOLLOW THEM.

COME ON, LET'S ATTACK THEM AFTER DARK TONIGHT.

LATER THAT NIGHT, A SUSPICIOUS CROWD SURROUNDS LOT'S HOUSE...

THOSE STRANGERS— BRING 'EM OUT!

NO! THEY ARE GUESTS IN MY HOUSE!

IT WILL BE WORSE FOR YOU, LOT, IF YOU DON'T SEND THEM OUT.

BUT, JUST AS THE MOB REACHES OUT FOR LOT, THE TWO STRANGERS PULL HIM INSIDE AND LOCK THE DOOR!

BREAK DOWN THE DOOR!

LET'S GET THEM!

OUTSIDE LOT'S HOUSE IN SODOM, THE MOB GOES WILD. RIOTERS HOWL FOR REVENGE AGAINST LOT AND THE STRANGERS WHO RESCUED HIM.

COME ON— WE'LL BREAK DOWN THE DOOR!

AS THE MEN PUSH AGAINST LOT'S DOOR, THE ANGELS STRIKE THE RIOTERS BLIND.

HELP! I CAN'T SEE!

MY EYES— WHO HIT ME?

INSIDE LOT'S HOUSE...

RUN FOR YOUR LIVES! THE LORD HAS SENT US TO DESTROY THIS WICKED CITY!

MY FAMILY— I MUST SAVE THEM!

BUT LOT'S SONS-IN-LAW ONLY LAUGH WHEN HE TRIES TO WARN THEM. THEY REFUSE TO LEAVE THE DOOMED CITY, SO, EARLY THE NEXT MORNING, THE TWO ANGELS LEAD LOT, HIS WIFE AND THEIR TWO DAUGHTERS AWAY. SUDDENLY ALL SODOM BURSTS INTO FLAME!

LOT'S WIFE STOPS...LOOKS BACK LONGINGLY... AND IS TURNED INTO A PILLAR OF SALT...SO ONLY LOT AND HIS TWO DAUGHTERS ESCAPE GOD'S PUNISHMENT.

DON'T LOOK BACK AT THE CITY—OR YOU WILL ALSO DIE!

I DON'T CARE WHAT GOD SAYS—I WANT TO GO BACK!

NEXT MORNING, ABRAHAM GOES TO THE HILLTOP TO WORSHIP—AND SEES THE SMOULDERING RUINS OF THE WICKED CITY...

AS SURELY AS NIGHT FOLLOWS DAY, DESTRUCTION FOLLOWS SIN. O GOD, HELP ME TO LEAD MY PEOPLE IN THE PATHS OF RIGHTEOUSNESS!

As Abraham takes his family far from Sodom he discovers that Sarah is pregnant. Sarah's son is born in their new home, Beer-sheba, near the desert.

ABRAHAM HAS NAMED HIS SECOND SON, ISAAC.

WHAT WILL BECOME OF ISHMAEL, HIS FIRST SON? HE MIGHT HAVE BEEN OUR RULER AFTER ABRAHAM, BUT NOW THE BABY, ISAAC, WILL RULE OUR PEOPLE.

I'M AFRAID THERE WILL BE TROUBLE.

SARAH AND HAGAR BECOME MORE JEALOUS DAY BY DAY. THEN AT THE BABY ISAAC'S FIRST FEAST...

SEE HOW CLUMSY LITTLE ISAAC IS!

ISHMAEL! BE QUIET!

SARAH IS ANGRY! WHAT WILL SHE DO?

HAGAR'S SON CAN'T MAKE FUN OF MINE! ABRAHAM, YOU MUST SEND ISHMAEL AND HAGAR AWAY, BEFORE THEY CAUSE TROUBLE IN THE TRIBE.

NIGHT AFTER NIGHT, ABRAHAM SEEKS GOD'S ANSWER TO HIS PROBLEM. FINALLY, HE KNOWS WHAT HE MUST DO.

EARLY ONE MORNING...

BECAUSE OF SARAH'S JEALOUSY, IT IS BETTER THAT YOU AND ISHMAEL LEAVE. HAVE NO FEAR, GOD WILL WATCH OVER YOU.

DAY AFTER DAY, THEY WANDER THROUGH THE BURNING SAND. ONE FEAR POUNDS IN HAGAR'S MIND.

WILL THE WATER HOLD OUT TILL WE FIND AN OASIS?

AT LAST THE DREADED MOMENT COMES...

THERE'S NO MORE WATER, MOTHER! I'M DYING OF THIRST!

I KNOW, SON. SO AM I. LIE DOWN IN THE SHADE OF THE BUSH.

O GOD, LET ME NOT SEE THE DEATH OF MY CHILD!

DEAD TIRED AND CHOKING WITH THIRST, HAGAR TURNS HER BACK ON HER SON, ISHMAEL... SHE CANNOT WATCH HIM DYING. SUDDENLY SHE HEARS A VOICE. IT'S GOD SAYING: "LIFT UP THE LAD, FOR I WILL MAKE HIM A GREAT NATION".

HAGAR STARTS TOWARD HER SON...

AND SEES A SPRING NEARBY.

WATER! WE WILL NOT DIE! O ISHMAEL, GOD HAS SAVED US!

KNOWING GOD IS WITH THEM, HAGAR AND ISHMAEL CONTINUE THEIR JOURNEY TO A PLACE IN THE WILDERNESS WHERE THEY BUILD A HOME. YEARS PASS—ISHMAEL MARRIES AN EGYPTIAN GIRL AND BECOMES THE HEAD OF A GREAT DESERT TRIBE.

Trouble
in the
Family

Isaac, the son of Abraham and Sarah, grows up and marries a beautiful woman named Rebekah. Years later they rejoice at the birth of their twin sons, Jacob and Esau.

UNDER ISAAC'S PEACEFUL LEADERSHIP, THE TRIBE CONTINUES TO GROW. THE PEOPLE ARE LOYAL, EVEN WHEN ISAAC MOVES THEM FROM PLACE TO PLACE TO AVOID WAR WITH NEIGHBORING TRIBES OVER WATER HOLES THAT ARE RIGHTFULLY HIS. BUT ISAAC FAILS TO SEE THE CONFLICT BETWEEN HIS OWN SONS.

WHICH ONE WILL RULE OUR TRIBE AFTER ISAAC?

ESAU—IT IS HIS BIRTHRIGHT BECAUSE HE WAS BORN FIRST.

WHEN ESAU RETURNS WITH FOOD, ISAAC PRAISES HIM.

ESAU IS A MIGHTY HUNTER.

MY TIME WILL COME —AND SOON!

JACOB BIDES HIS TIME... ONE MORNING, DURING A HOT SPELL, ESAU SETS OUT FOR A HUNTING TRIP...THIS IS THE CHANCE JACOB HAS BEEN WAITING FOR.

GAME WILL BE AT THE WATER HOLE, MILES AWAY. HE'LL BE TIRED AND HUNGRY AFTER THE LONG DAY'S HUNT. I'LL BE READY FOR HIM.

TOWARD SUNDOWN JACOB WAITS FOR HIS BROTHER OUTSIDE CAMP.

CAMP WITH ITS FOOD IS ONLY A SHORT DISTANCE AWAY, BUT ESAU IS SO HUNGRY HE CANNOT WAIT...

I SWEAR—THE BIRTHRIGHT IS YOURS. NOW, LET ME SIT DOWN AND EAT.

HERE, EAT ALL YOU WANT.

ESAU'S BIRTHRIGHT IS MINE! SOMEDAY **I** WILL INHERIT A DOUBLE PORTION OF MY FATHER'S WEALTH! **I** WILL RULE THE TRIBE OF MY FATHER!

BUT JACOB HAS A LONG TIME TO WAIT. HIS FATHER IS STILL STRONG AND POWERFUL. WHEN THE PASTURES DRY UP, THE TRIBE MOVES TO BETTER GRASSLANDS NEAR GERAR. THERE HE DIGS WELLS— BUT GIVES THEM UP RATHER THAN FIGHT WITH OTHER SHEPHERDS WHO CLAIM THEM. IN TIME THE KING OF GERAR RECOGNIZES THE STRENGTH AND GOODNESS OF ISAAC, WHO SACRIFICES HIS OWN RIGHTS TO KEEP WARS FROM STARTING. SO THE KING COMES TO ISAAC AND ASKS THAT THE TWO CHIEFTAINS PROMISE ALWAYS TO BE FRIENDS. BEFORE AN ALTAR TO GOD, THEY PLEDGE FRIENDSHIP. AND SO ISAAC WINS A GREATER VICTORY BY PEACE THAN BY FIGHTING.

PEACE-LOVING ISAAC IS NOT AWARE OF THE JEALOUS PLOT THAT IS BUILDING UP IN HIS OWN FAMILY.

FIND MY SON, ESAU. TELL HIM THAT I MUST SEE HIM.

ISAAC HAS GROWN OLD. HIS EYESIGHT IS FAILING. NOW HE DECIDES IT IS TIME TO GIVE HIS ELDEST SON THE BLESSING WHICH WILL INCLUDE RULING THE TRIBE.

YOU CALLED ME, FATHER?

YES, ESAU. I AM OLD AND TIRED—AND I DON'T KNOW HOW SOON I SHALL DIE. BRING ME SOME CHOICE VENISON AND I WILL GIVE YOU THE BLESSING THAT SEALS YOUR BIRTHRIGHT.

THE NEWS REBEKAH OVERHEARS SENDS HER RUNNING THROUGH THE CAMP...

FIND JACOB! TELL HIM TO COME TO HIS MOTHER'S TENT— AT ONCE! HURRY!

LISTEN, JACOB! YOUR FATHER IS GETTING READY TO GIVE ESAU THE BLESSING. YOU MUST GET THAT BLESSING, OR THE BIRTHRIGHT YOU GOT FROM ESAU MEANS NOTHING.

BUT WHAT CAN I DO?

BEFORE YOU AND YOUR BROTHER WERE BORN, THE LORD SPOKE TO ME AND SAID: "THE ELDER SHALL SERVE THE YOUNGER." BUT ESAU WILL SERVE YOU ONLY IF YOU ARE CHIEF OF THE TRIBE.

MY SKIN IS SMOOTH, BUT ESAU IS HAIRY. FATHER WILL TOUCH ME AND KNOW I AM NOT ESAU. WHAT CAN WE DO?

I HAVE THOUGHT OF THAT, TOO. HERE, PUT ON ESAU'S ROBE—THESE SKINS ON YOUR ARMS AND NECK WILL MAKE YOU FEEL LIKE ESAU.

BUT WHAT IF...

DO YOU WANT THE BIRTHRIGHT? THEN, DO AS I TELL YOU—IF THE PLAN FAILS, I WILL TAKE THE BLAME.

YOU ARE RIGHT, MOTHER. GIVE ME THE FOOD.

A SHORT TIME LATER, JACOB ENTERS HIS FATHER'S TENT.

FATHER, I HAVE BROUGHT THE MEAT YOU WANTED. EAT AND GIVE ME YOUR BLESSING.

HAVE YOU FOUND THE FOOD SO QUICKLY, MY SON?

THE LORD HELPED ME.

AH, YES, THE LORD HELPS THOSE WHO OBEY. COME NEAR ME THAT I MAY MAKE SURE YOU ARE MY ELDEST SON BEFORE I GIVE THE BLESSING.

STRANGE—THE VOICE IS THE VOICE OF JACOB; BUT THE HANDS ARE ESAU'S. ARE YOU TRULY MY SON ESAU?

I AM.

THE LIES HE HAS TOLD WEIGH HEAVILY ON JACOB'S MIND. HE TURNS AWAY WHILE HIS FATHER EATS OF THE BLESSING FEAST. IF JACOB IS TEMPTED TO TELL THE TRUTH, HE GIVES UP ALL THOUGHT OF IT WHEN HIS FATHER ASKS HIM TO KNEEL BEFORE HIM.

GOD GIVE THEE OF THE FATNESS OF THE EARTH...LET PEOPLE SERVE THEE...AND NATIONS BOW DOWN TO THEE...BE LORD OVER THY BRETHREN...CURSED BE EVERY ONE THAT CURSETH THEE, AND BLESSED BE HE THAT BLESSETH THEE.

NO SOONER IS THE BLESSING GIVEN, THAN JACOB RUSHES OUT OF HIS FATHER'S TENT.

MOTHER! THE BLESSING IS MINE! BUT WHAT WILL ESAU SAY?

NO MATTER WHAT ESAU SAYS, THE BLESSING IS YOURS. NOT EVEN YOUR FATHER CAN TAKE IT BACK NOW!

BUT WHILE JACOB AND HIS MOTHER ARE REJOICING, ESAU RETURNS.

59

ESAU PREPARES THE MEAT AND TAKES A LARGE TRAY OF IT TO HIS FATHER.

MY FATHER, EAT THE FOOD I HAVE BROUGHT YOU AND BLESS ME.

WHO ARE YOU?

WHO AM I?.. WHY, I AM YOUR SON—YOUR FIRST-BORN SON, ESAU. YOU TOLD ME TO BRING YOU THIS VENISON SO THAT YOU COULD GIVE ME YOUR BLESSING.

I HAVE BEEN DECEIVED! I HAVE GIVEN THE BLESSING TO ANOTHER!

OH, FATHER, BLESS ME ALSO! PLEASE BLESS ME!

I CAN'T—YOUR BROTHER HAS TAKEN YOUR BLESSING!

BUT, FATHER, HAVE YOU NO OTHER BLESSING FOR ME?

ONLY THIS, MY SON. BY THY SWORD SHALT THOU LIVE AND SERVE THY BROTHER...BUT THE TIME WILL COME WHEN YOU WILL BREAK HIS YOKE FROM YOUR NECK.

TREMBLING WITH RAGE, ESAU LEAVES HIS FATHER'S TENT...

I'LL KILL JACOB FOR THIS!

WITH ESAU'S THREAT TO KILL JACOB RINGING IN HER EARS, THE SERVANT GIRL RUNS TO REBEKAH'S TENT.

ESAU IS GOING TO KILL JACOB!

ESAU IS UPSET—TELL NO ONE WHAT YOU HAVE HEARD. FIND JACOB AND TELL HIM TO COME TO ME— AT ONCE!

YOU MUST GO AWAY UNTIL YOUR BROTHER'S ANGER COOLS. GO TO MY BROTHER, LABAN, IN HARAN. I WILL SEND FOR YOU WHEN IT IS SAFE TO RETURN.

WHAT WILL I TELL MY FATHER?

ONCE AGAIN, REBEKAH PAVES THE WAY FOR HER FAVORITE SON.

ISAAC, ESAU'S WIVES ARE A GREAT TROUBLE TO ME. LIFE WILL NOT BE WORTH LIVING FOR ME IF JACOB MARRIES A WOMAN OF THIS COUNTRY. IF ONLY HE COULD MARRY A GIRL FROM MY PEOPLE—REMEMBER HOW YOUR FATHER'S SERVANT FOUND ME AT MY FATHER'S HOUSE IN HARAN AND BROUGHT ME TO YOU?

61

ISAAC'S THOUGHTS GO BACK OVER THE YEARS TO THE DAY HE FIRST SAW REBEKAH. HE ALSO KNOWS THERE WILL BE TROUBLE BETWEEN HIS SONS. HE SENDS FOR JACOB.

ASHAMED, BUT FRIGHTENED BY ESAU'S ANGER, JACOB COMES TO HIS FATHER.

GO TO THY MOTHER'S BROTHER, LABAN, AND FIND A WIFE FROM AMONG HIS FAMILY. GOD BLESS YOU, MY SON.

A FEW HOURS LATER—AT THE EDGE OF CAMP...

GOOD-BY, MY SON. I'LL SEND WORD WHEN IT IS SAFE TO RETURN.

MY FATHER IS OLD—I MAY NEVER SEE HIM AGAIN. ESAU WANTS TO KILL ME. OH, MOTHER, YOU ARE THE ONLY ONE I WILL BE ABLE TO COME BACK TO!

ONE PUNISHMENT FOR THEIR DECEIT IS THAT REBEKAH AND JACOB NEVER SEE EACH OTHER AGAIN.

TRAVELING FARTHER AND FARTHER FROM HIS FAMILY AND FRIENDS, JACOB IS TORTURED BY LONELINESS. HE ESPECIALLY MISSES HIS MOTHER, WHO HAS ALWAYS PROTECTED AND ADVISED HIM. HE IS HAUNTED BY THE MEMORY OF HOW HE TRICKED HIS FATHER AND BROTHER.

AS NIGHT APPROACHES...

IT'S GETTING DARK...I'LL HAVE TO STOP HERE TONIGHT.

JACOB SOON FALLS ASLEEP...AND HE DREAMS OF A SHINING LADDER, REACHING UP TO HEAVEN. ON THE LADDER ARE ANGELS, GOING UP AND DOWN AS IF BRINGING HELP FROM GOD. AND JACOB HEARS GOD SPEAK TO HIM, PROMISING TO TAKE CARE OF HIM AND BRING HIM SAFELY HOME AGAIN.

THE NEXT MORNING JACOB AWAKENS, STILL AWED BY THE DREAM HE HAD.

SURELY GOD IS IN THIS PLACE—AND THIS IS THE GATE OF HEAVEN.

JACOB REALIZES THE WRONG HE HAS DONE. BUT HE KNOWS THAT GOD WILL HELP HIM IF HE OBEYS HIM. QUICKLY HE TURNS A STONE ON END FOR AN ALTAR AND WORSHIPS GOD. HE CALLS THE PLACE BETH-EL, WHICH MEANS "THE HOUSE OF GOD."

IF GOD WILL GO WITH ME, I'LL BE GOD'S MAN.

JACOB GOES ON HIS WAY A STRONGER, NOBLER YOUNG MAN BECAUSE HE HAS FOUND GOD. HE IS EAGER TO PUT BEHIND HIM THE DISHONESTY OF HIS PAST AND BECOME REALLY WORTHY OF GOD'S LOVE AND CARE.

Slave
Train to
Egypt

Many years pass. Jacob marries two wives, Rachel and Leah. Leah has six sons, but Jacob's favorite wife, Rachel, has only two, Joseph and Benjamin.

WHEN ISAAC DIES, JACOB TAKES OVER AS HEAD OF THE TRIBE. WORD IS SENT TO ESAU, WHO COMES TO HELP JACOB BURY THEIR FATHER. AS SOON AS ESAU LEAVES, JACOB CALLS HIS SONS TO HIM...

THERE IS NOT ENOUGH PASTURE LAND FOR ALL OF OUR FLOCKS. WE WILL TAKE SOME OF THEM TO SHECHEM.

MAY I GO WITH MY BROTHERS TO TEND THE FLOCKS?

NO, JOSEPH, STAY HERE WITH ME. I HAVE SOMETHING FOR YOU.

SEE HOW FATHER FAVORS JOSEPH!

HE ALWAYS HAS! NOW HE MAY TRAIN HIM TO RULE THE TRIBE.

I'LL NEVER TAKE ORDERS FROM JOSEPH!

WHEN THE OLDER SONS ARE GONE...

HERE, MASTER JOSEPH, IS THE COAT YOUR FATHER HAD MADE FOR YOU.

FOR ME! WHY IT'S JUST LIKE A CHIEFTAIN'S ROBE!

WHEN THE OLDER SONS RETURN, THEY ARE JEALOUS OF JOSEPH'S COAT. THEN HE TELLS THEM ABOUT HIS DREAMS...

LAST NIGHT I DREAMED WE WERE BINDING SHEAVES, AND ALL OF YOUR SHEAVES BOWED DOWN TO MINE.

BOW DOWN TO HIM? **NEVER!**

STILL LATER JOSEPH HAS ANOTHER DREAM...

I DREAMED THE SUN AND MOON AND STARS BOWED TO ME.

WHAT? SHALL YOUR PARENTS AND BROTHERS SERVE YOU?

JACOB SOON FORGETS HIS OWN ANGER TOWARD JOSEPH, BUT THE SECOND DREAM WHIPS THE OLDER BROTHERS' HATRED INTO A BURNING RAGE.

SEVERAL DAYS LATER THE BROTHERS ARE TENDING THE SHEEP SOME DISTANCE FROM CAMP, AND JACOB SENDS JOSEPH TO SEE HOW THEY ARE GETTING ALONG.

HERE COMES THE DREAMER.

I'VE HAD ENOUGH OF HIS TALK. LET'S GET RID OF HIM!

THE CARAVAN IS WELL OUT OF SIGHT BY THE TIME REUBEN RETURNS...

WHERE IS JOSEPH? WHAT HAVE YOU DONE TO HIM?

WE SOLD HIM TO SOME TRADERS. THEIR CARAVAN IS GOING TO EGYPT. HERE'S YOUR SHARE OF THE MONEY.

SOLD HIM? OH, NO! WHAT WILL YOU TELL FATHER?

WE'LL SMEAR JOSEPH'S COAT WITH GOAT'S BLOOD AND LET FATHER THINK HE WAS KILLED BY A LION.

BACK IN CAMP, THE BROTHERS CARRY OUT THEIR CRUEL PLAN.

WE FOUND THIS BLOODY COAT— IS IT..?

IT'S JOSEPH'S! A LION MUST HAVE KILLED HIM! OH, JOSEPH, MY SON, MY SON!

WHILE JACOB IS STILL MOURNING THE DEATH OF HIS BELOVED SON, JOSEPH IS SOLD AGAIN AS A SLAVE IN EGYPT.

LOOK— THIS BOY IS STRONG AND HANDSOME. HE'D MAKE A FINE SLAVE, EVEN IN THE KING'S PALACE. HOW MUCH AM I BID?

THIRTY SHEKELS!

I AM A SLAVE! O GOD, PLEASE HELP ME!

AND SO, JACOB'S FAVORITE SON BECOMES THE SLAVE OF POTIPHAR, CAPTAIN OF THE KING'S GUARD. BUT JOSEPH DOES NOT BEG FOR PITY. HE PUTS HIS TRUST IN GOD AND HOLDS HIS HEAD UP PROUDLY.

GOOD SLAVE FOR THIRTY SHEKELS!

HE DOESN'T HAVE THE MANNER OF A SERVANT. TELL ME MORE ABOUT HIM.

SOME TRADERS BROUGHT HIM DOWN FROM CANAAN. HE'S STRONG— INTELLIGENT, TOO!

AND HANDSOME! IN THE RIGHT CLOTHES, HE'D PASS FOR A PRINCE!

YEARS PASS, AND POTIPHAR MAKES JOSEPH MANAGER OF ALL OF HIS PROPERTY.

THINGS ARE BETTER WITH JOSEPH IN CHARGE.

HE PRAYS EVERY DAY, ASKING HIS GOD TO HELP HIM.

BUT JOSEPH'S SUCCESS ALSO LEADS TO TROUBLE. POTIPHAR'S WIFE FALLS IN LOVE WITH THE HANDSOME, YOUNG SLAVE. ONE DAY WHILE POTIPHAR IS AWAY...

JOSEPH, COME, SIT BESIDE ME. TELL ME WHERE YOU CAME FROM AND WHY YOU ARE IN EGYPT.

THANK YOU, BUT I HAVE WORK TO FINISH BEFORE POTIPHAR RETURNS.

MUST YOU ALWAYS THINK OF POTIPHAR?

HE IS MY MASTER— I WILL NOT BE UNTRUE TO HIM OR DISOBEY MY GOD.

NO MAN CAN SCORN ME—AND LIVE!

SHE BIDES HER TIME...WHEN POTIPHAR RETURNS SHE GREETS HIM WITH TEARS IN HER EYES, AND A LIE ON HER LIPS.

YOUR HEBREW SLAVE TRIED TO KISS ME! I SCREAMED AND HE LEFT...BUT HE DROPPED HIS ROBE. HERE— SEE IT!

I'LL THROW HIM IN PRISON FOR THIS!

BEFORE THE SUN SETS THAT DAY, JOSEPH IS CHAINED AND THROWN INTO THE KING'S PRISON.

HO—WHAT A HANDSOME PRISONER WE HAVE WITH US!

WHEN HE'S BEEN HERE AS LONG AS I HAVE, HE'LL FORGET WHAT IT'S LIKE TO WEAR SUCH FINE, CLEAN CLOTHES.

FALSELY ACCUSED, JOSEPH **FACES** HIS FIRST NIGHT IN PRISON. BUT HE IS NOT AFRAID, AN**D** HE IS NOT ALONE BECAUSE GOD IS WITH HIM. JOSEPH PRAYS... AS HE HAS DONE EVERY OTHER NIGHT IN HIS LIFE.

WHAT GOD CAN SAVE HIM NOW?

LEAVE HIM ALONE! HE IS BRAVER THAN THE REST OF US.

ONE LONG, HOT DAY FOLLOWS ANOTHER. THE PRISONERS QUARREL OVER FOOD—WATER— THE BEST PLACE TO SLEEP. ONE DAY A FIGHT BREAKS OUT...

STOP IT! FIGHTING WON'T HELP US.

EVEN IN PRISON GOD IS WITH JOSEPH. WHEN THE KEEPER OF THE JAIL LEARNS JOSEPH IS A LEADER, HE PUTS JOSEPH IN CHARGE OF THE OTHER PRISONERS.

ONE DAY THE KING'S BAKER AND BUTLER ARE THROWN INTO PRISON FOR OFFENDING THE KING. BOTH MEN HAVE DREAMS THAT TROUBLE THEM, AND THEY COME TO JOSEPH FOR HELP.

WHAT DO YOU THINK MY DREAM MEANT?

IN THREE DAYS YOU WILL BE THE KING'S BUTLER AGAIN. WHEN THAT TIME COMES, PLEASE SAY A GOOD WORD FOR ME.

NOW TELL ME WHAT MY DREAM MEANS.

I'M SORRY, BUT THE DREAM SHOWS YOU WILL BE HANGED, IN JUST THREE DAYS.

JOSEPH'S WORDS COME TRUE. THREE DAYS LATER, ONE MAN DIES, AND THE OTHER RETURNS TO SERVE THE KING. BUT HE FORGETS HIS PROMISE. TWO YEARS GO BY...

YOU CALLED, O KING?

YES. IS THERE NO ONE IN MY WHOLE KINGDOM WHO CAN TELL ME WHAT MY DREAM MEANS? I MUST FIND OUT...

O KING, I KNOW A HEBREW PRISONER WHO CAN TELL THE MEANING OF DREAMS. HE TOLD MINE!

BRING HIM TO ME—AT ONCE!

73

THE BUTLER WASTES NO TIME IN HAVING JOSEPH RELEASED FROM PRISON. HE KNEELS BEFORE THE PHARAOH OF EGYPT.

IS IT TRUE YOU CAN TELL THE MEANING OF DREAMS?

NOT I—BUT MY GOD GIVES THE ANSWER, O PHARAOH. TELL ME YOUR DREAM.

I SAW SEVEN FAT COWS COME OUT OF THE NILE RIVER. AFTER THEM CAME SEVEN LEAN COWS THAT ATE THE FAT ONES.

GOD IS WARNING YOU THAT THERE WILL BE SEVEN YEARS OF GOOD CROPS FOLLOWED BY SEVEN YEARS OF FAMINE.

LET PHARAOH APPOINT A WISE OFFICER TO STORE GRAIN DURING THE SEVEN GOOD YEARS. THEN THERE WILL BE FOOD FOR ALL DURING THE SEVEN YEARS OF FAMINE.

WHO IS WISER THAN YOU, SINCE GOD IS WITH YOU?

PHARAOH QUICKLY SUMMONS THE OFFICERS OF HIS COURT. AS THEY WATCH, HE PUTS HIS OWN RING ON JOSEPH'S FINGER.

I HAVE PUT YOU IN CHARGE OF ALL EGYPT. ONLY I, PHARAOH, WILL BE GREATER THAN YOU!

FROM THE THRONE ROOM, JOSEPH GOES TO HIS OWN ROOM AND KNEELS IN PRAYER, THANKING GOD FOR PROTECTION AND GUIDANCE.

JOSEPH ORDERS THE PEOPLE TO START PREPARING FOR THE FAMINE. HE BECOMES FAMOUS, AND ALL REJOICE WHEN HE MARRIES THE BEAUTIFUL DAUGHTER OF THE PRIEST OF ON.

I AM PROUD TO BE YOUR WIFE, JOSEPH. YOU HAVE DONE SO MUCH FOR OUR PEOPLE.

THERE IS MORE TO BE DONE, MY DEAR. THE YEARS OF PLENTY WILL PASS QUICKLY.

ALL TOO SOON, THE FAMINE BEGINS. AS IT CONTINUES, PEOPLE FROM OTHER COUNTRIES COME TO EGYPT SEEKING FOOD. ONE DAY TRIBESMEN FROM CANAAN ENTER JOSEPH'S CITY...

IN ORDER TO BUY GRAIN, THEY APPEAR BEFORE THE GOVERNOR OF EGYPT. THEY BOW BEFORE HIM...

MY BROTHERS! THEY DO NOT RECOGNIZE ME AFTER ALL THESE YEARS!

75

THE TEN SONS OF JACOB STAND BEFORE THE GOVERNOR OF EGYPT—NOT KNOWING THAT HE IS JOSEPH, THE BROTHER THEY SOLD INTO SLAVERY YEARS BEFORE. BUT JOSEPH RECOGNIZES HIS HALF-BROTHERS—AND DECIDES TO FIND OUT WHETHER THEY HAVE LEARNED TO BE KIND AND MERCIFUL.

YOU ARE SPIES!

NO, MY LORD! WE ARE TEN OF THE SONS OF THE GREAT CHIEFTAIN, JACOB. HE SENT US TO BUY GRAIN.

TEN SONS? HOW MANY MORE SONS DOES YOUR FATHER HAVE?

HE HAD TWELVE—THE YOUNGEST, BENJAMIN, IS HOME WITH OUR FATHER. THE OTHER ONE DIED LONG AGO!

I STILL SAY YOU ARE SPIES. GUARD —TAKE THEM TO PRISON!

WHY SHOULD HE THINK WE'RE SPIES?

I DON'T KNOW—BUT IT WAS STRANGE THAT THE GOVERNOR WANTED TO KNOW HOW MANY SONS OUR FATHER HAD.

ON THE THIRD DAY THE BROTHERS ARE ONCE MORE BROUGHT BEFORE JOSEPH.

YOU MAY BUY GRAIN— BUT TO MAKE SURE YOU ARE NOT SPIES, I WILL HOLD ONE OF YOU IN PRISON UNTIL YOUR YOUNGEST BROTHER IS BROUGHT TO ME.

ME—IN PRISON?

HOURS PASS...THE BROTHERS TRY TO UNDERSTAND WHAT HAS HAPPENED—BUT NEVER ONCE DO THEY SUSPECT THAT THEIR BROTHER JOSEPH IS THE GOVERNOR.

THIS MUST BE PUNISHMENT FOR WHAT WE DID TO JOSEPH LONG AGO.

I TOLD YOU NOT TO HARM HIM!

HAS IT TAKEN YOU ALL THESE YEARS TO REGRET THE EVIL YOU DID THAT DAY?

THE ONE BROTHER SIMEON IS QUICKLY BOUND AND TAKEN TO PRISON AS A HOSTAGE. FRIGHTENED AND EAGER TO LEAVE EGYPT, THE OTHER BROTHERS HURRY TO THE STOREHOUSE FOR GRAIN.

PAY ME FIRST— THEN I'LL FILL YOUR SACKS.

THE GRAIN SACKS FILLED, THE BROTHERS LEAVE EGYPT AT ONCE. THAT NIGHT AS THEY SET UP CAMP...

LOOK! THE MONEY I PAID FOR THE GRAIN!

IT'S A TRAP! I TELL YOU THERE'S SOMETHING MYSTERIOUS ABOUT EVERYTHING THAT'S HAPPENED SINCE WE CAME TO EGYPT!

I'D NEVER GO BACK EXCEPT—

EXCEPT THAT WE LEFT SIMEON THERE IN PRISON. AND BENJAMIN IS THE ONLY ONE WHO CAN SET HIM FREE.

WHO KNOWS— MAYBE NEXT TIME WE COME THE GOVERNOR WILL KEEP BENJAMIN— OR ONE OF US!

FOR DAYS, AS THE CARAVAN TRAVELS NORTHEAST THE BROTHERS WORRY ABOUT WHAT THEIR FATHER WILL SAY.

BACK HOME, THEY PROUDLY SHOW THEIR FATHER HOW MUCH GRAIN THEY HAVE BROUGHT...

LOOK— THE MONEY IS IN MY SACK, TOO!

AND MINE!

WHAT IS THIS? MONEY IN YOUR GRAIN SACKS— AND WHERE IS SIMEON?

IN—IN PRISON IN EGYPT, AND...

SIMEON IN PRISON? WHY? SPEAK UP. WHAT HAPPENED?

THE WHOLE TRIP WAS VERY STRANGE, FATHER. THE GOVERNOR SAID WE WERE SPIES. HE PUT US ALL IN PRISON, THEN HE RELEASED ALL OF US BUT SIMEON. SIMEON HAS TO STAY THERE—UNTIL WE TAKE BENJAMIN TO EGYPT.

BENJAMIN TO EGYPT? NEVER! MY SON JOSEPH HAS BEEN DEAD THESE MANY YEARS—NOW SIMEON IS LOST TO ME. I WILL NOT PART WITH BENJAMIN.

BUT FATHER— WHAT ABOUT SIMEON?

YES, WHAT ABOUT SIMEON? AND WHAT ABOUT **US** IF THE GRAIN RUNS OUT AND WE HAVE TO GO TO EGYPT AGAIN? WE CAN'T GO WITHOUT BENJAMIN!

THE GRAIN IS USED SPARINGLY, BUT ONE DAY JACOB'S HUNGRY TRIBE HAS TO FACE THE TRUTH...

THE GRAIN IS ALMOST GONE— WHAT SHALL WE DO?

JACOB, THE OLD CHIEFTAIN, FACES A HARD DECISION...

BUT WHY SHOULD THE GOVERNOR OF EGYPT HOLD SIMEON IN PRISON UNTIL HE SEES BENJAMIN? WHAT DOES HE WANT WITH MY YOUNGEST SON?

NOBODY KNOWS. BUT IF I DON'T GO, SIMEON WILL DIE IN PRISON—AND WE WILL STARVE. I MUST GO, FATHER—I MUST!

BENJAMIN IS RIGHT.

THEN—GO. TAKE DOUBLE THE AMOUNT OF MONEY FOR GRAIN—TAKE GIFTS TO THE GOVERNOR. AND MAY GOD BE MERCIFUL TO US!

DAYS LATER, JACOB'S SONS LEAD THEIR PACK ANIMALS THROUGH THE GATES OF THE EGYPTIAN CITY.

DON'T WORRY, BENJAMIN, WE'LL DO EVERYTHING WE CAN TO PROTECT YOU.

I AM NOT AFRAID—GOD WILL TAKE CARE OF US HERE JUST AS HE DOES IN OUR FIELDS AT HOME.

THEY ENTER THE COURTYARD OF THE GOVERNOR... WHO THEY DO NOT KNOW IS THEIR BROTHER JOSEPH.

WE ARE THE SONS OF JACOB COME AGAIN FOR GRAIN. WHEN WE RETURNED HOME FROM BUYING FOOD, WE FOUND MONEY IN OUR SACKS. WE HAVE BROUGHT THAT MONEY WITH US—AND MORE TO BUY MORE GRAIN.

MY MASTER KNOWS YOU HAVE COME. WAIT HERE—

SIMEON!

O BENJAMIN, THANK GOD YOU CAME!

YOU ARE ALL RIGHT?

YES, BUT I WAS AFRAID YOU'D NEVER COME. THE PRISON WAS DARK AND LONELY. ALL I COULD THINK OF WAS THE EVIL I HAD DONE IN MY LIFE.

FORGET THE PAST, SIMEON. WE ARE ELEVEN BROTHERS AND WE WILL STICK TOGETHER.

THEN—TO THEIR SURPRISE—THE BROTHERS ARE LED INTO A GREAT BANQUET HALL. THE GOVERNOR OF EGYPT STANDS WAITING...

BUT EVEN AS THEY WONDER, THE GOVERNOR HAS THE BROTHERS SERVED — GIVING THE LARGEST PORTION TO BENJAMIN. IT IS A SIGN OF GREAT HONOR.

DO YOU SEE THAT?

AT LEAST BENJAMIN IS SAFE!

THE BANQUET ENDS; THE NEXT MORNING THE BROTHERS BUY THEIR GRAIN AND LEAVE. BUT THEY ARE HARDLY OUT OF THE CITY BEFORE A CHARIOT OVERTAKES THEM.

STOP! ONE OF YOU HAS STOLEN MY MASTER'S SILVER CUP!

YOUR MASTER'S CUP? WE ARE INNOCENT! SEARCH US IF YOU WILL.

IF THE CUP IS FOUND, THE MAN IN WHOSE SACK IT IS HIDDEN SHALL BECOME MY MASTER'S SLAVE!

ONE BY ONE THE SACKS ARE SEARCHED... AT LAST THE OFFICER OPENS BENJAMIN'S...

THE CUP!

84

THE ONE IN WHOSE BAG THE CUP WAS FOUND SHALL BE MY SERVANT—THE REST OF YOU MAY RETURN TO YOUR FATHER.

IF BENJAMIN DOES NOT RETURN HOME, OUR FATHER WILL DIE OF GRIEF. LET ME BE YOUR SLAVE INSTEAD OF BENJAMIN.

FOR A MOMENT THERE IS SILENCE. THEN THE GOVERNOR TURNS TO HIS GUARDS.

GO! LEAVE ME ALONE WITH THESE MEN.

THE FRIGHTENED BROTHERS WAIT. FINALLY JOSEPH SPEAKS...

I CAN'T KEEP THE SECRET ANY LONGER—I AM YOUR BROTHER, JOSEPH! YOU SOLD ME AS A SLAVE MANY YEARS AGO. GOD HAS BLESSED ME RICHLY...NOW WE ARE TOGETHER AGAIN.

JOSEPH!

HE MUST HATE US... WHAT WILL HE DO NOW?

I BELIEVE IT WAS GOD'S WILL THAT I CAME TO EGYPT TO SAVE YOUR LIVES—AND THE LIVES OF OTHERS—IN THIS FAMINE.

WE DON'T DESERVE GOD'S MERCY. JOSEPH, CAN YOU FORGIVE US?

I FORGAVE YOU ALL, YEARS AGO. BUT I HAD TO BE SURE YOU HAD CHANGED. WHEN YOU SHOWED YOUR LOYALTY AND YOUR LOVE FOR OUR FATHER, I KNEW YOU HAD.

THE FAMINE WILL LAST FIVE YEARS MORE—GO BACK HOME AND BRING OUR FATHER TO BE NEAR ME, AND I WILL PROVIDE FOR ALL OF YOU.

THANK GOD FOR A BROTHER LIKE YOU.

WHEN PHARAOH HEARS THE NEWS, HE CALLS FOR JOSEPH...

GIVE YOUR BROTHERS WAGONS SO THEY CAN BRING THEIR FAMILIES AND YOUR FATHER TO LIVE IN EGYPT.

LOADED WITH SUPPLIES AND GIFTS THE HAPPY CARAVAN SETS OUT FOR HOME. WHEN THEY APPROACH JACOB'S CAMP, SOME OF THE BROTHERS RUN AHEAD TO TELL THE GOOD NEWS.

FATHER! FATHER! WE HAVE NEWS!

JOSEPH IS ALIVE! HE'S THE GOVERNOR OF ALL EGYPT!

JACOB RISES TO GREET HIS SONS...BUT WHEN HE HEARS JOSEPH'S NAME HE SINKS BACK...

JOSEPH ALIVE? I CAN'T BELIEVE IT!

Jacob gathers his family and all their flocks and moves to Egypt to be reunited with his long lost son.

Escape
from
Pharaoh

For years after Joseph's death the Egyptians treat the Hebrews well. But new rulers come to the throne. . . .

THIS COULD MEAN TROUBLE FOR US.

THE NEW KING DOES NOT LIKE US HEBREWS. HE HAS FORGOTTEN THAT IT WAS OUR ANCESTOR JOSEPH WHO SAVED EGYPT FROM FAMINE.

FROM HIS ROYAL YACHT ON THE NILE, THE KING FROWNS AS HE WATCHES THE HEBREW SHEPHERDS WITH THEIR RICH FLOCKS.

THERE ARE TOO MANY HEBREWS IN EGYPT! IN CASE OF WAR THEY MIGHT TURN AGAINST US. HOW CAN WE KEEP THEM FROM CAUSING TROUBLE?

NEXT DAY THE KING INSPECTS A NEW BUILDING PROJECT.

WE NEED WORKMEN. THOUSANDS MORE THAN WE HAVE.

I HAVE IT! THE HEBREWS WILL WORK AS SLAVES. IT WILL SAVE US MONEY AND THEY WON'T BE ABLE TO CAUSE TROUBLE.

SO FROM DAYLIGHT TO DARK HEBREW MEN AND BOYS ARE DRIVEN FROM THEIR HOMES AND FORCED TO WORK UNDER WHIP-CRACKING SLAVE DRIVERS.

BUT THE HEBREWS ARE STRONG.

WE WORK THEM HARDER EVERY DAY, BUT THERE ARE MORE HEBREWS THAN BEFORE. THE KING WILL NOT BE HAPPY ABOUT THIS...

WHEN THE KING HEARS THE REPORT...

I'LL TAKE CARE OF THE SLAVES! THROW EVERY HEBREW BOY BABY IN THE RIVER!

THE CRUEL ORDER IS CARRIED OUT. HEBREW MOTHERS AND FATHERS RISK THEIR LIVES TO PROTECT THEIR SONS...BUT THE KING'S MEN NEVER GIVE UP THEIR SEARCH.

NIGHT AFTER NIGHT ONE HEBREW FATHER HURRIES HOME FROM WORK—AFRAID THAT THE SOLDIERS HAVE VISITED HIS HOME.

O GOD, HELP ME SAVE OUR BOY FROM THE EGYPTIANS.

THERE'S MIRIAM! A SIGN THAT MY LITTLE SON IS STILL SAFE.

QUICKLY THE FATHER ENTERS THE HOUSE—AND BOLTS THE DOOR.

SURELY GOD IS WITH US—OUR BABY IS THREE MONTHS OLD AND STILL PHARAOH'S SOLDIERS HAVE NOT FOUND HIM.

GOD WILL HELP ME FIND A WAY TO SAVE OUR SON!

NEXT DAY THE MOTHER SETS ABOUT PREPARING A LITTLE BASKET.

KEEP WATCH, MIRIAM, I'M ALMOST FINISHED.

THEN, CAREFULLY AVOIDING THE EGYPTIAN SOLDIERS, SHE TAKES THE BASKET AND HER TINY SON TO THE RIVER.

BROTHER'S BASKET FLOATS LIKE A LITTLE BOAT!

KEEP WATCH OVER HIM, MIRIAM. OH, MY SON, IT TEARS MY HEART TO SEND YOU AWAY. MAY GOD WATCH OVER YOU AND PROTECT YOU ALWAYS...

MIRIAM HIDES IN THE BULRUSHES AND WATCHES...

THE PRINCESS! WILL SHE SEE THE BABY'S BASKET?

LOOK—WHAT A STRANGE LITTLE BASKET! I WONDER WHAT'S INSIDE IT?

THE MAID BRINGS THE BASKET TO THE PRINCESS, WHO OPENS IT.

A HEBREW BABY! LISTEN TO HIM CRY! WE MUST FIND SOMEBODY TO FEED AND CARE FOR THE CHILD.

AT THIS POINT MIRIAM STEPS FORTH...

SHALL I FIND A HEBREW NURSE FOR THE BABY?

YES—BRING HER TO ME AS SOON AS YOU CAN.

MOTHER! COME AT ONCE! THE PRINCESS HAS FOUND OUR BABY— AND SHE WANTS A HEBREW NURSE FOR HIM.

GOD HAS ANSWERED MY PRAYER, MIRIAM. MY SON WILL BE SAFE WITH THE PRINCESS.

AT THE RIVER'S EDGE—

TAKE THIS BABY, AND CARE FOR HIM. IF ANYONE QUESTIONS YOU, SEND WORD TO ME AT ONCE.

SO THE HEBREW BABY IS RETURNED TO HIS OWN HOME —BUT NOW UNDER THE PROTECTION OF THE KING'S DAUGHTER. THAT NIGHT THE MOTHER, FATHER, MIRIAM AND YOUNG AARON KNEEL AND PRAY...

O GOD, WE THANK THEE FOR SAVING OUR LITTLE SON. HELP US TO TRAIN HIM TO SERVE THEE!

THE LITTLE BOY LIVES IN HIS HOME UNTIL HE IS ABOUT FOUR YEARS OLD. THEN HIS MOTHER TAKES HIM TO THE PALACE TO LIVE WITH THE PRINCESS WHO HAS ADOPTED HIM.

HE WILL BE _MY_ SON. HIS NAME WILL BE MOSES BECAUSE THAT IS LIKE THE WORD THAT MEANS "TO DRAW OUT", AND I DREW HIM OUT OF THE WATER.

YEARS PASS, AND THE BOY MOSES LIVES THE LIFE OF A YOUNG PRINCE IN PHARAOH'S PALACE. HE LEARNS TO WRITE AND READ. LATER HE GOES TO COLLEGE. ONE DAY HE DRIVES THROUGH THE CITY...

...TO A PLACE WHERE HEBREW SLAVES ARE WORKING. AS HE WATCHES THE SLAVES TOIL, HE IS STARTLED BY A MAN'S SCREAM...

MOSES JUMPS FROM HIS CHARIOT TO INVESTIGATE...AND FINDS AN EGYPTIAN GUARD BEATING A HEBREW SLAVE.

IN SUDDEN ANGER MOSES STRIKES OUT HARD—

LOOK! HE KILLED THE GUARD!

THE NEXT DAY MOSES RETURNS. WHEN HE SEES TWO HEBREWS FIGHTING, HE TRIES TO STOP THEM.

WHY DO YOU FIGHT AMONG YOURSELVES?

WHO MADE YOU A JUDGE OVER US? ARE YOU GOING TO KILL ME AS YOU DID THAT EGYPTIAN?

IF PHARAOH HEARS OF THIS HE WILL ACCUSE ME OF BEING A TRAITOR. THERE IS ONLY ONE THING FOR ME TO DO, AND I MUST DO IT NOW...

LATER THAT DAY IN THE PALACE...

PRINCE MOSES KILLED AN EGYPTIAN GUARD FOR BEATING A HEBREW SLAVE!

FIND THE TRAITOR—AND KILL HIM!

BUT PHARAOH'S ORDERS ARE TOO LATE...MOSES HAS A HEAD START ON THE SOLDIERS WHO CHASE HIM. HE ESCAPES—AND AFTER LONG, HARD RIDING REACHES THE LAND OF MIDIAN.

ONE EVENING HE RESTS BY A WELL.

GET AWAY FROM HERE UNTIL WE WATER OUR SHEEP!

NO— WE WERE HERE FIRST. YOU LEAVE US ALONE!

STAND BACK—THE GIRLS _WERE_ HERE FIRST!

THE COWARDLY SHEPHERDS RETREAT—AND MOSES HELPS THE GIRLS WATER THEIR FLOCKS.

WHEN THE GIRLS RETURN TO THEIR CAMP ONE OF THEM TELLS THEIR FATHER WHAT HAPPENED AT THE WELL

WHERE IS THIS MAN? FIND HIM AND INVITE HIM TO EAT WITH US.

I AM ZIPPORAH. MY FATHER, JETHRO, INVITES YOU TO EAT WITH US.

MOSES ACCEPTS THE INVITATION—AND THAT NIGHT AFTER SUPPER...

I NEED A SHEPHERD—WHY DON'T YOU STAY WITH US?

THANK YOU, I WILL.

THIS WILL BE A GOOD PLACE TO HIDE FROM PHARAOH.

MOSES STAYS WEEKS AND THEN MONTHS. HE MARRIES ZIPPORAH AND IN TIME THEY HAVE TWO SONS.

GERSHOM HANDLES HIS SLING VERY WELL.

HE WILL MAKE A GOOD SHEPHERD— LIKE HIS FATHER.

YEAR AFTER YEAR THE FLOCKS OF JETHRO INCREASE. BUT ONE YEAR THE GRASSES DRY UP AND MOSES LEADS HIS SHEEP TO PASTURES NEAR THE MOUNTAIN OF SINAI.

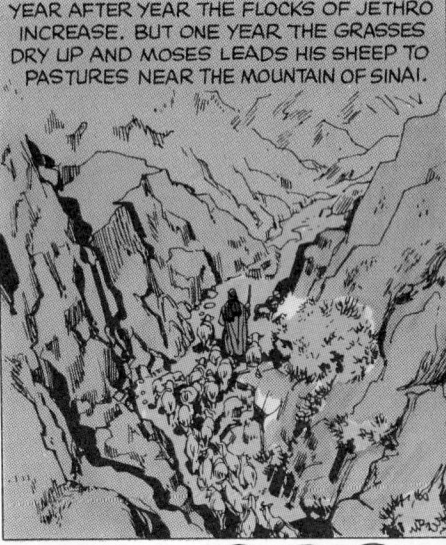

BUT MOSES CANNOT FORGET THE HEBREW PEOPLE IN EGYPT.

I WONDER IF PHARAOH IS STILL ALIVE... AND WHAT HAS BECOME OF MY SISTER MIRIAM AND MY BROTHER AARON?

HE WONDERS, TOO, ABOUT THE HEBREW SLAVES STILL STRUGGLING UNDER THE WHIPS OF EGYPTIAN RULERS. ONE DAY HE LOOKS UP TO SEE A STRANGE SIGHT ON MOUNT SINAI.

A BUSH ON FIRE— YET IT IS NOT DESTROYED!

HE STEPS CLOSER—THEN STOPS. A VOICE FROM THE FIERY BUSH CALLS OUT **"MOSES!"**

THE VOICE CONTINUES: "I AM THE GOD OF YOUR FATHERS...GO DOWN TO EGYPT, TELL PHARAOH TO SET THE HEBREWS FREE."

WHO AM _I_ TO SPEAK TO THE PHARAOH OF EGYPT?

HERE AM I!

MOSES IS AFRAID—AFRAID OF THE PHARAOH OF EGYPT, AFRAID HE CANNOT SPEAK PROPERLY— AFRAID THE HEBREW PEOPLE WILL NOT BELIEVE HIM. BUT GOD ASSURES HIM: "GO— YOUR BROTHER AARON WILL SPEAK FOR YOU. I WILL BE WITH YOU."

ONCE AGAIN MOSES STARTS TOWARD THE BUSH, BUT THE SAME VOICE WARNS HIM: "DO NOT COME NEARER... TAKE OFF YOUR SHOES, FOR THE GROUND ON WHICH YOU STAND IS HOLY GROUND."

MOSES OBEYS. HE RETURNS TO CAMP AND TELLS HIS FATHER-IN-LAW WHAT GOD HAS CALLED HIM TO DO.

GO IN PEACE. GOD WILL STRENGTHEN YOU, AS HE HAS PROMISED.

AND SO MOSES SETS OUT FOR EGYPT WITH HIS WIFE AND SONS.

MEANTIME...IN THE SLAVE HUTS OF EGYPT, THE HEBREWS ARE ASKING GOD TO HELP THEM.

WHILE AARON, THE BROTHER OF MOSES, IS PRAYING, GOD SPEAKS TO HIM: "GO INTO THE WILDERNESS TO MEET YOUR BROTHER."

AARON IS SURPRISED AT THE STRANGE COMMAND. BUT, LIKE MOSES, HE OBEYS. SOON HE IS ALONE IN THE WILDERNESS.

MOSES HAS BEEN GONE FROM EGYPT FOR MANY YEARS. WILL HE KNOW ME? DOES HE KNOW I'M COMING? I WONDER WHAT GOD WANTS US TO DO?

AARON'S QUESTIONS ARE SOON ANSWERED. HE MEETS HIS BROTHER AT MOUNT SINAI.

MOSES!

AARON—I HAVE BEEN WATCHING FOR YOU!

HOW DID YOU KNOW I WAS COMING?

GOD TOLD ME YOU WOULD COME —TO HELP ME.

QUICKLY, MOSES EXPLAINS THAT GOD HAS CALLED THEM TO LEAD THE HEBREWS OUT OF SLAVERY IN EGYPT.

WHEN MOSES AND AARON DEMAND THE RELEASE OF THE HEBREW SLAVES, PHARAOH IS FURIOUS—AND MAKES THE SLAVES WORK HARDER THAN BEFORE. IN ANGER THEY TURN AGAINST MOSES. MOSES SEEKS GOD'S HELP AND IS TOLD TO VISIT PHARAOH AGAIN.

SHOW ME HOW POWERFUL YOUR GOD IS.

WHEN THIS ROD STRIKES THE GROUND, IT WILL BECOME A SERPENT.

AARON'S WORDS COME TRUE, BUT PHARAOH ONLY LAUGHS.

YOU ARE CLEVER, BUT MY MAGICIANS CAN DO THE SAME THING.

PHARAOH CALLS FOR HIS OWN MAGICIANS. THEY TOO THROW DOWN THEIR RODS—WHICH BECOME SERPENTS.

SEE?

BUT WHILE PHARAOH WATCHES, THE SERPENT OF AARON DEVOURS THE SERPENTS OF THE EGYPTIAN MAGICIANS. PHARAOH IS STUNNED...BUT HE REFUSES TO ADMIT THAT MOSES' GOD IS MORE POWERFUL THAN THE GODS OF EGYPT.

AGAIN MOSES SEEKS GOD'S HELP...AND AGAIN GOD TELLS HIM WHAT TO DO. IN THE MORNING MOSES AND AARON MEET PHARAOH ON THE BANK OF THE RIVER NILE.

WHAT ARE _YOU_ DOING HERE?

BECAUSE YOU WILL NOT LET THE HEBREWS GO, THE RIVER WILL BE TURNED TO BLOOD.

AT MOSES' COMMAND, AARON STRIKES THE WATER WITH HIS ROD AND THE WATER TURNS RED.

I DON'T DARE BATHE IN THAT BLOODY STREAM!

WHEN WOMEN COME TO WASH THEIR CLOTHES IN THE RIVER, THEY ARE TURNED BACK. MEN HAVE TO DIG WELLS TO GET DRINKING WATER. FINALLY THE RIVER IS CLEAR AGAIN, BUT STILL PHARAOH WILL NOT LISTEN TO MOSES' PLEA. AND SO GOD SENDS A DIFFERENT PLAGUE...

IN THE STREETS OF THE CITY...

FROGS— MILLIONS OF THEM... EVERYWHERE!

AND IN THE EGYPTIAN HOMES...

EE-EEK! A FROG IN MY BREAD DOUGH!

EVEN IN THE PALACE...

FROGS IN MY BED! I CAN'T STAND THIS— SEND FOR MOSES AND AARON.

ASK YOUR GOD TO TAKE AWAY THE FROGS, AND I WILL LET THE HEBREWS GO.

IT SHALL BE AS YOU SAY.

BUT WHEN THE FROGS ARE GONE, PHARAOH BREAKS HIS PROMISE. SO STILL ANOTHER PLAGUE DESCENDS ON EGYPT...

FIRST THERE COMES A PLAGUE OF LICE— LATER GREAT SWARMS OF BITING FLIES FILL THE AIR...

ONCE AGAIN PHARAOH PROMISES TO FREE THE HEBREWS. BUT WHEN THE FLIES DISAPPEAR, HE BREAKS HIS WORD. THEN DISEASE BREAKS OUT AMONG THE CATTLE, AND PHARAOH AND HIS PEOPLE SUFFER FROM PAINFUL BOILS.

FATHER, WERE THE SLAVE DRIVERS CRUEL TODAY?

THEY ARE ALWAYS CRUEL, SON, BUT RIGHT NOW THEY ARE SUFFERING FROM TERRIBLE BOILS WHILE WE ARE STRONG AND HEALTHY.

STILL PHARAOH KEEPS THE HEBREWS IN EGYPT. SO A TERRIBLE STORM STRIKES.

HAILSTONES AS BIG AS MY FIST!

THROUGHOUT THE LAND, THE EGYPTIAN FARMERS WATCH THE STORM WITH TERROR.

OUR CROPS ARE RUINED...

...BUT NO HAIL FALLS ON THE LAND WHERE THE HEBREWS LIVE.

LATER, MILLIONS OF LOCUSTS SWARM THROUGH THE LAND. AFTER A STRONG WIND BLOWS THEM AWAY, THE DAY BECOMES AS DARK AS NIGHT.

IT'S SO DARK—I'M AFRAID.

WILL THESE TERRIBLE TROUBLES NEVER CEASE?

AFTER THREE DAYS OF DARKNESS PHARAOH CALLS FOR MOSES AND AARON.

I'LL LET YOUR PEOPLE GO—BUT YOUR SHEEP AND CATTLE MUST REMAIN IN EGYPT.

NO!. NOT A HOOF SHALL BE LEFT BEHIND.

THEN THEY SHALL STAY! AND YOU—GET OUT OF HERE. IF I SEE YOUR FACE AGAIN, YOU'LL DIE!

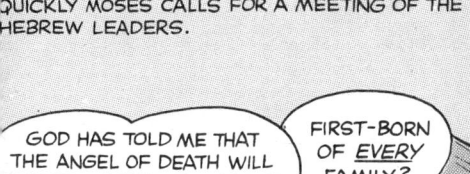

QUICKLY MOSES CALLS FOR A MEETING OF THE HEBREW LEADERS.

GOD HAS TOLD ME THAT THE ANGEL OF DEATH WILL CROSS EGYPT—TAKING THE FIRST-BORN OF EVERY FAMILY...

FIRST-BORN OF *EVERY* FAMILY?

WAIT! WE WILL BE SAVED— IF WE OBEY GOD!

MOSES HAS TOLD THE PEOPLE THAT AT A CERTAIN HOUR DEATH WOULD STRIKE THE FIRST-BORN IN ALL EGYPT. BUT HE HAS ALSO TOLD THEM HOW TO PROTECT THEIR FAMILIES...

NINE TIMES PHARAOH HAS BROKEN HIS PROMISE TO LET US GO— WHAT WILL HE DO THIS TIME?

SURELY THIS WILL BRING OUR RELEASE FROM SLAVERY.

WHY ARE YOU PUTTING LAMB'S BLOOD ON OUR DOOR-POSTS?

GOD TOLD MOSES IT WOULD BE A SIGN FOR THE ANGEL OF DEATH TO PASS OVER OUR HOUSE.

THAT EVENING, EVERY HEBREW FAMILY GETS READY TO LEAVE EGYPT. THEY EAT A FEAST CALLED THE PASSOVER BECAUSE THE ANGEL OF DEATH WAS PASSING OVER THEIR HOMES.

THIS DOUGH·HAS NO YEAST—WE'LL HAVE TO EAT FLAT BREAD CAKES.

BE READY FOR THE SIGNAL TO MARCH!

...AND AT MIDNIGHT THE ANGEL OF DEATH STRIKES ALL EGYPT.

IN THE PALACE...

YOUR SON IS DEAD, O PHARAOH! AND MESSENGERS BRING WORD THAT THE FIRST-BORN OF EVERY EGYPTIAN HOME HAS DIED SUDDENLY TONIGHT.

MY SON!

SUMMON MOSES AND AARON— AT ONCE!

IT'S TOO LATE—TOO LATE! MY SON IS DEAD.

THIS TIME PHARAOH DOES NOT BARGAIN ABOUT CATTLE OR SHEEP.

TAKE YOUR PEOPLE— TAKE YOUR CATTLE AND GET OUT OF EGYPT. SERVE YOUR GOD AS YOU HAVE SAID.

THE ORDER TO MARCH IS GIVEN...IMMEDIATELY THE SLAVES RUSH OUT FROM THEIR SLAVE HUTS, AND MEET AT A CAMP IN THE COUNTRY.

WE'RE FREE! WE'RE FREE!

THANK GOD, MY CHILDREN WILL NOT BE SLAVES IN EGYPT!

The Giant Killer

Many years after the Hebrew people escape from Egypt they settle in the Promised Land where God has led them. Cities spring up and the crops grow. Soon jealous enemy tribes try to take over the land. The people ask the prophet Samuel for a king to protect them. However, their new king turns from good to evil.

TWICE KING SAUL DELIBERATELY DISOBEYS GOD. THE PROPHET, SAMUEL, HAS TOLD HIM THAT HIS KINGDOM WILL BE TAKEN FROM HIM. SAUL IS AFRAID—AND AT TIMES HIS MIND BECOMES UNBALANCED. WHEN HIS ADVISORS TELL HIM ABOUT DAVID, A YOUNG SHEPHERD, WHO SINGS AND PLAYS A HARP, SAUL SENDS FOR HIM. DAVID ARRIVES AT THE PALACE...

THE KING IS VERY ILL TODAY—SO HE MAY BE DANGEROUS. NEVER TAKE YOUR EYES OFF HIM.

QUIETLY DAVID ENTERS THE KING'S ROOM AND BEGINS TO PLAY...SAUL STARES AT HIM WILDLY... BUT DAVID CONTINUES TO PLAY AND SING OF HIS FAITH IN GOD.

LAST KING SAUL RELAXES AND [F]ALLS QUIETLY ASLEEP. AFTER THAT [D]AVID IS OFTEN CALLED TO THE [P]ALACE. HIS MUSIC QUIETS SAUL'S [T]ORTURED MIND—AND IN TIME THE [K]ING SEEMS WELL AGAIN.

AND WHEN WORD COMES THAT THE PHILISTINES ARE PREPARING FOR AN ATTACK, SAUL LEADS HIS ARMY AGAINST THEM. DAVID'S THREE OLDEST BROTHERS JOIN THE KING'S FORCES.

ONE EVENING DAVID COMES IN FROM THE FIELDS TO FIND HIS FATHER BUSY PACKING FOOD.

THIS IS FOR YOUR BROTHERS. I WANT YOU TO TAKE IT TO THEM.

I'LL LEAVE RIGHT AWAY. WHAT'S THE LATEST NEWS FROM THE FRONT?

NOT GOOD, AND I'M WORRIED.

WHEN DAVID REACHES THE ISRAELITE CAMP, HE FINDS THE SOLDIERS STRANGELY QUIET.

WHAT'S THE MATTER?

114

WHEN DAVID REACHES THE ISRAELITE CAMP, HE FINDS THAT NO ISRAELITE SOLDIER IS BRAVE ENOUGH TO ACCEPT THE PHILISTINE GIANT'S CHALLENGE TO FIGHT. DAVID IS ANGRY—BUT SO IS ELIAB, HIS BIG BROTHER...

WHAT ARE **YOU** DOING HERE? WHY AREN'T YOU HOME WHERE YOU BELONG—TAKING CARE OF THE SHEEP?

FATHER SENT ME HERE WITH FOOD FOR YOU—NOW **YOU** TELL ME WHY NO ONE HAS ACCEPTED GOLIATH'S CHALLENGE TO FIGHT?

EVER SINCE THE PROPHET SAMUEL CHOSE DAVID INSTEAD OF HIM, ELIAB HAS BEEN FILLED WITH JEALOUSY...NOW IT BURSTS INTO THE OPEN.

YOU'RE JUST A SHOW-OFF.

I'M NOT AFRAID. I'LL FIGHT THE GIANT.

MEANWHILE IN KING SAUL'S TENT...

EVERY DAY THAT GIANT DEFIES US. I HAVE OFFERED A HANDSOME REWARD—EVEN MY DAUGHTER IN MARRIAGE—BUT NOT ONE SOLDIER IN MY WHOLE ARMY WILL ACCEPT THE CHALLENGE.

115

O KING—THERE IS ONE OUTSIDE WHO ACCEPTS, BUT—

BRING HIM HERE AT ONCE!

DAVID ENTERS—BUT SAUL DOES NOT REMEMBER THE SHEPHERD WHO PLAYED FOR HIM.

A SHEPHERD BOY! YOU CAN'T FIGHT A GIANT!

THE LORD WHO HELPED ME KILL A LION AND A BEAR WILL HELP ME NOW.

MAYBE YOU'RE RIGHT—AT LEAST YOU HAVE COURAGE. GO, AND THE LORD BE WITH THEE. YOU CAN WEAR MY OWN ARMOR.

I CAN'T WEAR THIS—I'M NOT USED TO FIGHTING IN ARMOR. BESIDES, MY PLAN IS NOT TO DEFEND MYSELF, BUT TO ATTACK!

WITH ONLY HIS STAFF AND A SLING, DAVID GOES OUT TO MEET THE PHILISTINE GIANT. THE ARMIES OF BOTH CAMPS WATCH THEIR CHAMPIONS AS THEY FACE EACH OTHER.

AM I A DOG, THAT YOU COME AT ME WITH STICKS AND STONES?

I'LL GIVE YOUR FLESH TO THE WILD BEASTS.

YOU COME WITH A SWORD, A SPEAR AND A SHIELD — BUT I COME IN THE NAME OF GOD, WHO WILL GIVE ME THE VICTORY.

THE GIANT LAUGHS — BUT DAVID WHIRLS HIS SLING, TAKES CAREFUL AIM, AND LETS THE STONE FLY...

FOR FORTY DAYS THE PHILISTINE GIANT, GOLIATH, CHALLENGES THE ISRAELITES TO FIGHT. BUT NOT ONE SOLDIER IN ALL OF KING SAUL'S ARMY IS BRAVE ENOUGH TO ACCEPT THE CHALLENGE, UNTIL DAVID, THE YOUNG SHEPHERD, OFFERS TO MEET THE GIANT WITH ONLY A STAFF, A SLING—AND HIS FAITH IN GOD! EVEN WHILE DAVID WHIRLS HIS SLING, THE GIANT LAUGHS, BUT THE STONE HITS ITS MARK...AND THE GIANT FALLS!

GOLIATH'S DEAD!

IN TERROR, THE PHILISTINES FLEE FOR THEIR LIVES. SPURRED ON BY THIS SUDDEN TURN OF EVENTS, THE EXCITED ISRAELITES CHASE THE PHILISTINES BACK TO THEIR OWN LAND.

TRIUMPHANTLY, KING SAUL AND HIS VICTORIOUS SOLDIERS RETURN HOME...THE WOMEN RUSH OUT OF THE CITIES TO GREET THEM AND SING THEIR PRAISES.

SAUL HAS SLAIN HIS THOUSANDS—AND DAVID HIS TEN THOUSANDS!

Trial
by Fire

THE STORY OF WHAT HAPPENED TO A ROYAL CAPTIVE FROM JUDAH BEGINS WHEN DANIEL AND HIS THREE FRIENDS—SHADRACH, MESHACH, AND ABEDNEGO—ENTER THE CITY OF BABYLON AT THE END OF THEIR 900 MILE MARCH FROM JERUSALEM.

WHAT DO YOU THINK THEY'LL DO TO US, DANIEL?

I DON'T KNOW, SHADRACH. BUT I AM SURE OF THIS, GOD IS WITH US.

SOON AFTER THE PRISONERS REACH THE CITY, DANIEL AND SEVERAL OTHERS ARE BROUGHT BEFORE AN OFFICER OF KING NEBUCHADNEZZAR.

AS NOBLES FROM JERUSALEM, YOU WILL BE GIVEN A CHANCE TO TRY OUT FOR POSITIONS IN THE KING'S COURT. BUT I WARN YOU-- ONLY THE SMARTEST AND STRONGEST CAN PASS OUR TESTS.

FOR DAYS THE YOUNG MEN ARE GIVEN EXAMINATIONS TO TEST THEIR PHYSICAL STRENGTH AND MENTAL ALERTNESS.

THIS IS THE LAST TEST. BY TOMORROW YOU WILL KNOW HOW MANY PASSED.

WHAT IF WE FAIL?

WE'VE DONE OUR BEST-- THAT'S ALL WE CAN DO.

122

THE NEXT DAY...

YOU HAVE ALL PASSED -- NOW YOU'LL BE GIVEN THREE YEARS TO STUDY UNDER OUR WISE MEN. AFTER THAT THE KING HIMSELF WILL CHOOSE THOSE BEST QUALIFIED TO BE HIS ADVISERS.

O GOD, THANK YOU. HELP US TO PASS THESE NEW TESTS SO THAT WE MAY ADVISE THE KING IN A WAY THAT WILL PLEASE YOU.

THE YOUNG MEN ARE TAKEN AT ONCE TO THE PALACE TO BEGIN THEIR STUDIES. THEY ARE GIVEN THE BEST OF EVERYTHING --EVEN FOOD FROM THE KING'S TABLE.

THANK YOU, BUT WE CANNOT EAT THIS MEAT AND DRINK THIS WINE. OUR HEBREW LAWS FORBID IT. GIVE US PLAIN FOOD AND WATER, PLEASE.

BUT IT'S THE KING'S ORDER -- WE DARE NOT DISOBEY. I LIKE YOU, DANIEL, BUT I DON'T WANT TO GET INTO TROUBLE.

GIVE US A TEN-DAY TRIAL. LET US EAT OUR FOOD AND THEN SEE IF WE ARE NOT STRONGER THAN THE OTHERS.

THE TEST IS MADE, AND AT THE END OF TEN DAYS, THERE'S NO DOUBT--DANIEL AND HIS FRIENDS NOT ONLY **LOOK** STRONGER, THEY **ARE** STRONGER.

AT THE END OF THREE YEARS, THE YOUNG MEN ARE BROUGHT BEFORE THE KING. HE TALKS WITH EACH ONE, THEN MAKES HIS DECISION.

I HAVE CHOSEN THESE FOUR--DANIEL, SHADRACH, MESHACH, AND ABEDNEGO -- TO SERVE AS MY ADVISERS.

THERE IS NONE TO EQUAL THEM, SIR.

KING NEBUCHADNEZZAR IS FURIOUS! HIS WISE MEN CANNOT TELL HIM WHAT HE HAS DREAMED. SO HE ORDERS ALL OF THEM PUT TO DEATH-- INCLUDING DANIEL AND HIS THREE FRIENDS, SHADRACH, MESHACH, AND ABEDNEGO. DANIEL ASKS FOR PERMISSION TO SPEAK TO THE KING.

O KING, GIVE ME TIME AND I WILL TELL YOU WHAT YOU DREAMED.

YOU HAVE UNTIL TOMORROW AT THIS HOUR-- BUT NOT ONE MINUTE MORE.

DANIEL RUSHES BACK TO HIS FRIENDS WITH THE GOOD NEWS.

BUT, DANIEL, NO MAN ON EARTH CAN DO WHAT YOU HAVE PROMISED TO DO.

YOU ARE RIGHT-- NO MAN CAN DO IT, BUT GOD CAN. AND WE WILL ASK HIM TO GIVE US THE ANSWER.

125

AS THE FOUR YOUNG HEBREWS PRAY, A VISION COMES TO DANIEL.

O GOD, THANK YOU FOR MAKING THE DREAM KNOWN TO ME.

THE NEXT DAY --

HAVE YOU COME TO ASK FOR MORE TIME -- OR CAN YOU TELL ME MY DREAM?

GOD IN HEAVEN HAS REVEALED YOUR DREAM TO ME.

YOU SAW A MIGHTY STATUE -- ITS HEAD WAS MADE OF GOLD AND ITS FEET OF CLAY. THEN YOU SAW A LARGE STONE STRIKE AT THE FEET OF THE STATUE AND BREAK IT INTO MANY PIECES.

YES! YES! THAT'S RIGHT. BUT WHAT DOES IT MEAN?

THE HEAD OF GOLD STANDS FOR YOU AND YOUR GREAT KINGDOM, O KING. OTHER LESSER KINGDOMS WILL FOLLOW. BUT AFTER THEY FALL, GOD WILL SET UP A KINGDOM WHICH SHALL NEVER BE DESTROYED.

YOUR GOD IS A GOD ABOVE ALL GODS. AND YOU SHALL BE RULER OF THE PROVINCE OF BABYLON -- OVER ALL THE WISE MEN WHOSE LIVES YOU SAVED THIS DAY.

126

DANIEL RELAYS THE GOOD NEWS TO HIS HEBREW FRIENDS.

THE KING HAS MADE ME RULER OVER BABYLON AND EACH OF YOU HAS AN IMPORTANT OFFICE IN THE KINGDOM.

THAT'S WONDERFUL!

BUT THE NEWS DOES NOT PLEASE THE KING'S OTHER ADVISERS.

SO THE KING HAS PUT THIS YOUNG HEBREW OVER **US!** WE MUST GET RID OF HIM.

NOT NOW-- HE'S TOO POWERFUL! BUT IF WE CAN TURN THE KING AGAINST DANIEL'S FRIENDS, WE MIGHT BE ABLE TO CAUSE DANIEL TROUBLE.

THEIR OPPORTUNITY COMES WHEN THE KING BUILDS A STATUE AND ORDERS HIS OFFICIALS TO WORSHIP IT--OR BE THROWN INTO A FIERY FURNACE.

THE KING IS PLAYING RIGHT INTO OUR HANDS --HE DOESN'T KNOW THAT HEBREWS WILL WORSHIP ONLY THEIR GOD.

DANIEL HOLDS TOO HIGH A POSITION FOR ANY ONE OF US TO REPORT ON HIM-- BUT NOT HIS FRIENDS...

RIGHT--AND TOMORROW WHEN THE TRUMPET SOUNDS FOR ALL MEN TO BOW BEFORE THE STATUE, WE'LL KEEP OUR EYES ON SHADRACH, MESHACH, AND ABEDNEGO.

AT KING NEBUCHADNEZZAR'S COMMAND, A GIANT STATUE--90 FEET HIGH--IS BUILT ON THE PLAINS OF DURA. ALL OF THE OFFICIALS OF BABYLON ARE ORDERED TO WORSHIP IT. THE HOUR OF WORSHIP COMES--THE MOMENT FOR WHICH THE KING'S JEALOUS ADVISERS HAVE BEEN WAITING...

THE MUSICIANS HAVE TAKEN THEIR PLACES. THE SIGNAL WILL SOON BE GIVEN-- THE ONE THAT MEANS DEATH TO DANIEL'S FRIENDS--SHADRACH, MESHACH, AND ABEDNEGO!

MUSIC FILLS THE AIR-- SOLEMNLY THE OFFICIALS OF BABYLON BOW DOWN AND WORSHIP THE GOLDEN STATUE--ALL BUT SHADRACH, MESHACH, AND ABEDNEGO.

SEE? THEY REFUSE TO BOW DOWN!

EAGERLY, THE JEALOUS ADVISERS REPORT TO THE KING.

O KING, THREE OF YOUR HEBREW OFFICIALS HAVE DEFIED YOU. THEY REFUSE TO WORSHIP YOUR STATUE.

WHAT? HAVE THEM BROUGHT TO ME AT ONCE!

WORSHIP THE STATUE -- OR BE THROWN INTO THE FIERY FURNACE. AND TELL ME -- WHAT GOD CAN SAVE YOU FROM THAT?

IF WE ARE CAST INTO THE FIRE, THE GOD WHOM WE SERVE WILL BE ABLE TO DELIVER US! BUT EVEN IF WE MUST DIE, WE WILL NOT WORSHIP AN IDOL.

HEAT THE FURNACE -- SEVEN TIMES HOTTER THAN EVER BEFORE -- AND THROW THEM IN IT!

THE THREE HEBREWS ARE QUICKLY BOUND AND THROWN INTO THE RAGING FIRE.

129

BUT WHEN THE KING LOOKS INTO THE FURNACE...

THEY'RE ALIVE! NOT EVEN TOUCHED BY THE FLAMES! AND, DIDN'T WE CAST **THREE** INTO THE FIRE?

WE DID, O KING.

BUT I SEE **FOUR**! AND THE FOURTH LOOKS LIKE SOMEONE FROM HEAVEN.

SHADRACH! MESHACH! ABEDNEGO! COME OUT!

131

In the
Lions' Den

Nebuchadnezzar, the Babylonian king who brought the Jews to his land, has died. His successor, Belshazzar, does not respect the one, true God. He is so sure of his own wisdom that ...

HE LAUGHS AT TWO GREAT THREATS TO HIS KINGDOM: ANGRY PRIESTS WHO ARE TURNING AGAINST HIM, AND THE APPROACH OF THE MIGHTY PERSIAN ARMY. INSTEAD, HE PREPARES A GREAT FEAST TO WHICH HE INVITES A THOUSAND GUESTS...

THE PARTY IS AT ITS MERRIEST WHEN SUDDENLY BELSHAZZAR STARES AT A PLACE HIGH ON THE BANQUET WALL. HE TURNS PALE -- HIS HANDS TREMBLE...

LOOK! ON THE WALL! WHAT IS IT? WHAT DOES IT MEAN?

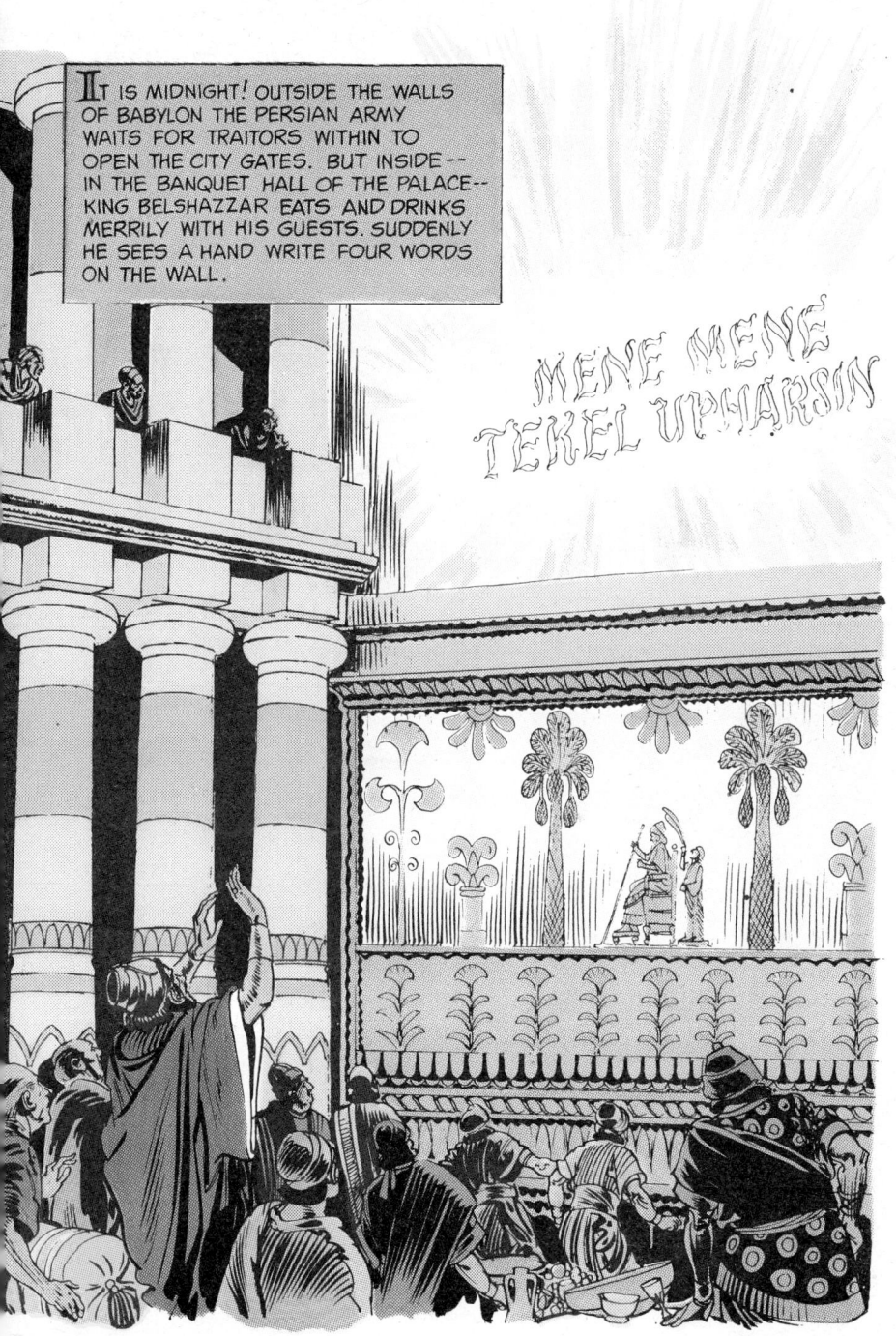

It IS MIDNIGHT! OUTSIDE THE WALLS OF BABYLON THE PERSIAN ARMY WAITS FOR TRAITORS WITHIN TO OPEN THE CITY GATES. BUT INSIDE -- IN THE BANQUET HALL OF THE PALACE-- KING BELSHAZZAR EATS AND DRINKS MERRILY WITH HIS GUESTS. SUDDENLY HE SEES A HAND WRITE FOUR WORDS ON THE WALL.

MENE MENE TEKEL UPHARSIN

TERRIFIED, BELSHAZZAR CALLS FOR HIS ADVISERS TO EXPLAIN THE WORDS, BUT THEY CANNOT. WHEN THE KING'S MOTHER HEARS THE EXCITEMENT IN THE BANQUET HALL SHE RUSHES TO HER SON.

MY SON, THERE'S A MAN IN YOUR KINGDOM NAMED DANIEL WHO CAN INTERPRET DREAMS. CALL HIM.

DANIEL! YES! YES! BRING HIM HERE AT ONCE!

NOT A SOUND IS HEARD IN THE GREAT BANQUET HALL UNTIL DANIEL APPEARS BEFORE THE KING.

TELL ME WHAT THOSE WORDS MEAN AND YOU SHALL BE SECOND ONLY TO ME IN ALL BABYLON.

O KING, THEY ARE A WARNING FROM GOD. YOU HAVE BEEN MEASURED AND FOUND LACKING IN THE QUALITIES OF A RULER. YOUR KINGDOM WILL BE GIVEN TO THE PERSIANS

I DON'T BELIEVE YOUR MESSAGE, BUT I'LL KEEP MY PROMISE. HERE, THIS CHAIN MAKES YOU NEXT TO ME IN ALL THE KINGDOM. NOW, ON WITH THE FEAST!

AS BELSHAZZAR SPEAKS, PERSIAN SOLDIERS SUDDENLY FILL THE HALL--AND TAKE HIM PRISONER.

SOLDIERS? WHERE DID THEY COME FROM? MY GUARDS! WHERE ARE MY GUARDS

BEFORE MORNING THE CITY IS IN THE HANDS OF THE ENEMY. BELSHAZZAR IS KILLED. DANIEL IS BROUGHT BEFORE DARIUS, THE COMMANDER, WHO RECOGNIZES DANIEL'S ABILITY AS A LEADER.

YOU WILL RULE OVER MY NOBLES AS LONG AS YOU OBEY ME.

DARIUS FINDS DANIEL VERY WISE AND OFTEN TURNS TO HIM FOR ADVICE.

DARIUS HAS APPOINTED DANIEL RULER OVER ALL OF US.

WE MUST GET RID OF HIM-- AND I KNOW JUST HOW TO DO IT!

O KING, YOUR NOBLES, WHO HONOR YOU ABOVE ALL, BEG YOU TO SIGN THIS LAW SO THAT **EVERYONE** WILL HONOR YOU. IT FORBIDS ANYONE TO BOW DOWN TO ANY GOD OR MAN BUT YOU, FOR THIRTY DAYS.

IF YOU WANT SUCH A LAW, I'LL SIGN IT.

137

DARIUS SIGNS THE LAW. WHEN IT IS ANNOUNCED, THE JEALOUS NOBLES HURRY DOWN THE STREET TO WATCH DANIEL'S WINDOW.

SEE--DANIEL PRAYS TO HIS GOD JUST AS WE EXPECTED!

GOOD-- NOW TO TELL DARIUS.

O KING, HAVE YOU NOT SIGNED A LAW FOR A MAN TO BE THROWN TO THE LIONS IF HE BOWS BEFORE ANYONE BUT YOU?

I HAVE--AND THE LAW OF THE PERSIANS CANNOT BE CHANGED!

DANIEL HAS BROKEN YOUR LAW. THREE TIMES A DAY HE PRAYS TO HIS GOD-- IN FRONT OF A WINDOW WHERE ALL CAN SEE!

DANIEL, MY FRIEND!

I SEE IT NOW-- MY NOBLES HAVE USED ME TO CONDEMN HIM TO DEATH!

SEAL THE DEN WITH A STONE SO THAT EVERYONE WILL KNOW I AM ENFORCING THE LAW.

IF ONLY I COULD CHANGE THIS ONE LAW TO SAVE MY FRIEND.

THAT NIGHT THE KING CAN NEITHER EAT NOR SLEEP. HE PACES UP AND DOWN HIS ROOM -- THINKING OF DANIEL.

AT DAYBREAK HE RUSHES TO THE LIONS' DEN.

ROLL AWAY THAT STONE!

DANIEL! DANIEL! DID YOUR GOD PROTECT YOU?

MY GOD HAS SHUT THE LIONS' MOUTHS!

THE KING IS OVERJOYED, AND ORDERS A ROPE THROWN DOWN, AND DANIEL IS PULLED OUT OF THE DEN. THEN HE SENDS FOR THE NOBLES WHO PLOTTED DANIEL'S DEATH.

YOU SENT DANIEL TO THE LIONS -- NOW WE'LL SEE HOW **YOU** LIKE IT!

GUARDS! THROW THEM INTO THE DEN!

EN DARIUS ISSUES A DECREE...

I, DARIUS, COMMAND ALL PEOPLE IN THIS KINGDOM TO HONOR THE GOD THAT DANIEL WORSHIPS AND SERVES.

AND FOR THE REST OF HIS LIFE, DANIEL HELPS TO RULE BABYLON, THE COUNTRY HE ENTERED AS A CAPTIVE. AGAINST ALL ODDS, HE BOLDLY STANDS FOR GOD -- AND GOD REWARDS HIM.

141

The King
Is Born

The Persian rulers send the Jews back to their land. Over the years the people rebuild their cities, but are again conquered by foreign powers. Their only hope is a prophecy that says God will one day send a deliverer.

THE WORLD INTO WHICH JESUS CAME

HERE, OLD MAN, CARRY THIS FOR ME.

FOR ALMOST SIXTY YEARS PALESTINE, THE HOME OF THE JEWS, HAS BEEN RULED BY THE MIGHTY ROMAN EMPIRE. TO MAINTAIN THEIR CONTROL, THE ROMANS APPOINTED HEROD, A CLEVER BUT CRUEL MAN, TO RULE THE LAND. THE JEWS HATE HIM -- AND THE ROMAN OFFICIALS WHO COME TO HIS COURT. THE TIME IS NOW 6 B.C....

THAT CHEST IS TOO HEAVY FOR SUCH AN OLD MAN.

THE ROMANS DON'T CARE.

HOURS LATER THE OLD MAN REACHES HOME...

GRANDFATHER! WHAT'S THE MATTER?

A ROMAN SOLDIER MAD HIM CARRY A HEAVY CHEST TO HEROD' PALACE.

145

THAT AFTERNOON--AS THE JEWS IN JERUSALEM GATHER IN THE TEMPLE FOR PRAYER -- AN OLD PRIEST, ZACHARIAS, ENTERS THE HOLY PLACE TO PRAY AND OFFER INCENSE.

THIS IS THE GREATEST DAY IN MY LIFE. AFTER ALL THESE YEARS IT IS FINALLY MY TURN TO OFFER INCENSE ON GOD'S HOLY ALTAR.

HE STAYS SO LONG IN THE SECRET ROOM THAT THE PEOPLE BEGIN TO WONDER.

ZACHARIAS' PRAYER IS LONGER THAN THAT OF MOST PRIESTS.

HE IS A GOOD MAN. IT'S TOO BAD HE HAS NO SON TO TAKE HIS PLACE.

AT LAST ZACHARIAS COMES OUT AND FACES THE PEOPLE -- BUT HE *CANNOT* SPEAK!

WHAT HAPPENED IN THE HOLY PLACE OF GOD?

ZACHARIAS, THE AGED PRIEST, HAS NOT SPOKEN A WORD SINCE HE ENTERED THE HOLY PLACE·OF THE TEMPLE TO OFFER INCENSE. MOST OF THE PEOPLE IN JERUSALEM BELIEVE HE SAW A VISION, BUT ZACHARIAS MAKES NO EXPLANATION. HE COMPLETES HIS TIME OF SERVICE IN THE TEMPLE, AND RETURNS TO HIS HOME IN THE HILLS OF JUDAH. HIS WIFE, ELISABETH, MEETS HIM AT THE DOOR...

ZACHARIAS! WHAT IS WRONG? WHY DON'T YOU SPEAK TO ME?

QUICKLY ZACHARIAS WRITES HIS ANSWER AND HANDS IT TO ELISABETH TO READ.

WHILE I WAS PRAYING IN THE HOLY PLACE, AN ANGEL SPOKE TO ME. HE TOLD ME THAT WE WOULD HAVE A SON. HIS NAME WILL BE JOHN, AND HE WILL PREPARE OUR PEOPLE FOR THE DELIVERER. FROM GOD.

147

A SON! AND HE WILL PREPARE THE WAY FOR GOD'S CHOSEN ONE!

BUT, ZACHARIAS, WHY DO YOU WRITE THIS INSTEAD OF TELLING ME?

ZACHARIAS WRITES A SECOND MESSAGE AND GIVES IT TO HIS WIFE.

GOD FORGIVE ME. I DOUBTED THE ANGEL'S MESSAGE, AND HE TOLD ME I WOULD NOT BE ABLE TO SPEAK UNTIL THE MESSAGE CAME TRUE.

OVERJOYED--AND AWED BY THE GREAT TRUST GOD HAS PLACED IN THEM-- ZACHARIAS AND ELISABETH PREPARE FOR THE BIRTH OF THEIR SON. IN THE MONTHS THAT PASS THEY OFTEN READ TOGETHER THE PARTS OF SCRIPTURE THAT TELL ABOUT GOD'S PROMISES TO HIS PEOPLE.

AS THE AGED PRIEST AND HIS WIFE WAIT FOR THE COMING OF THEIR SON, THE ANGEL GABRIEL APPEARS TO ELISABETH'S COUSIN MARY, WHO IS ENGAGED TO JOSEPH, A CARPENTER, IN NAZARETH.

DO NOT BE AFRAID, MARY. GOD HAS CHOSEN YOU TO BE THE MOTHER OF HIS SON. HIS NAME WILL BE "JESUS." HE WILL BE A KING WHOSE REIGN WILL NEVER END.

I AM THE LORD'S SERVANT AND I WILL DO WHATEVER HE SAYS.

MARY TELLS NO ONE OF THE ANGEL'S MESSAGE, BUT IN A FEW DAYS SHE GOES TO THE CARPENTER SHOP TO SEE JOSEPH.

I HAVE DECIDED TO GO AND VISIT MY COUSIN, ELISABETH.

IN JUDAH? I HATE TO HAVE YOU GO ALONE, MARY. IF ONLY THE PERIOD OF OUR ENGAGEMENT WERE OVER AND WE WERE MARRIED. THEN I COULD TAKE YOU THERE.

BUT, MARY LEAVES NAZARETH ALONE.

THE ANGEL SAID THAT ELISABETH IS GOING TO HAVE A SON, TOO. IT WILL BE GOOD TO TALK WITH HER.

AND WHEN SHE REACHES HER COUSIN...

MARY, HOW WONDERFULLY GOD HAS BLESSED YOU! BUT, TELL ME, WHY HAS THE MOTHER OF MY LORD COME TO VISIT ME?

FROM THIS GREETING MARY KNOWS THAT ELISABETH SHARES HER WONDERFUL SECRET. JOYFULLY SHE SINGS ALOUD HER PRAISE TO GOD.

MY SOUL DOTH MAGNIFY THE LORD... FOR HE THAT IS MIGHTY HATH DONE TO ME GREAT THINGS; AND HOLY IS HIS NAME.

149

THE DAYS PASS SWIFTLY IN THE HOME OF THE OLD PRIEST ZACHARIAS. HIS WIFE, ELISABETH AND HER YOUNG COUSIN, MARY, SPEND MANY HOURS TALKING ABOUT THE SONS GOD HAS PROMISED THEM. WHEN ELISABETH AND ZACHARIAS' CHILD IS BORN, NEIGHBORS AND RELATIVES COME TO SEE HIM.

HOW PROUD ZACHARIAS MUST BE TO HAVE A SON TO BEAR HIS NAME.

HE IS PROUD TO HAVE A SON, BUT, THE CHILD'S NAME IS JOHN.

JOHN? THEN YOU AREN'T NAMING HIM FOR ANYONE IN YOUR FAMILY?

ZACHARIAS -- WHO HAS NOT BEEN ABLE TO SPEAK A WORD SINCE HE DOUBTED THE ANGEL'S MESSAGE ABOUT THE BIRTH OF HIS SON -- MOTIONS FOR A TABLET. QUICKLY HE WRITES HIS ANSWER, AND HANDS IT TO THE WOMAN TO READ.

HIS NAME IS JOHN.

SO THE BABY IS NAMED ACCORDING TO THE INSTRUCTIONS OF THE ANGEL -- AND AT THAT MOMENT ZACHARIAS IS ABLE TO SPEAK.

BLESSED BE THE LORD GOD OF ISRAEL; FOR HE HATH VISITED AND REDEEMED HIS PEOPLE... AND THOU, CHILD, SHALT BE CALLED THE PROPHET OF THE HIGHEST: FOR THOU SHALT GO BEFORE THE FACE OF THE LORD TO PREPARE HIS WAYS.

ON THEIR WAY HOME THE PEOPLE TALK ABOUT THE STRANGE EVENTS CONNECTED WITH THE BIRTH OF ZACHARIAS' SON.

THE NAME JOHN -- WHAT DOES IT MEAN?

IT MEANS, "GOD HAS BEEN GRACIOUS." GOD MUST HAVE A SPECIAL PURPOSE FOR THAT CHILD.

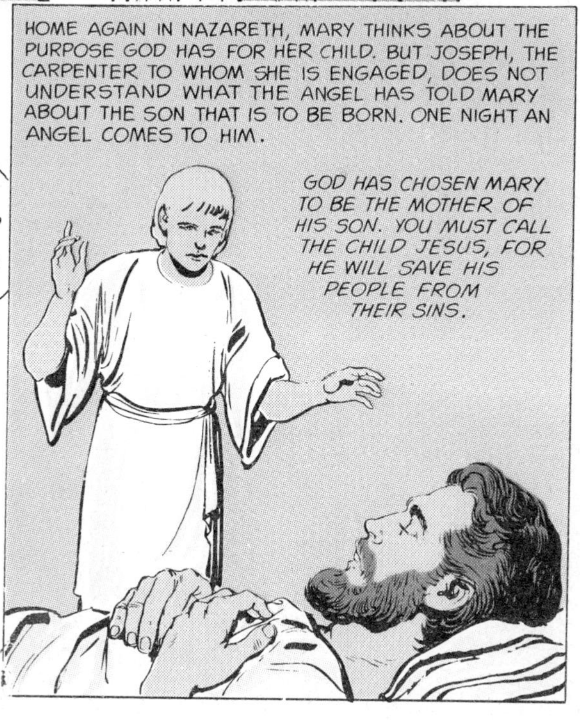

HOME AGAIN IN NAZARETH, MARY THINKS ABOUT THE PURPOSE GOD HAS FOR HER CHILD. BUT JOSEPH, THE CARPENTER TO WHOM SHE IS ENGAGED, DOES NOT UNDERSTAND WHAT THE ANGEL HAS TOLD MARY ABOUT THE SON THAT IS TO BE BORN. ONE NIGHT AN ANGEL COMES TO HIM.

GOD HAS CHOSEN MARY TO BE THE MOTHER OF HIS SON. YOU MUST CALL THE CHILD JESUS, FOR HE WILL SAVE HIS PEOPLE FROM THEIR SINS.

EARLY THE NEXT MORNING, JOSEPH HURRIES TO SEE MARY.

O MARY, IN A DREAM LAST NIGHT AN ANGEL TOLD ME THAT YOU ARE TO BE THE MOTHER OF THE LORD. I SEE NOW THAT GOD HAS CHOSEN ME TO TAKE CARE OF YOU AND YOUR SON.

SO MARY AND JOSEPH ARE MARRIED, AND MOVE INTO JOSEPH'S HOUSE BESIDE THE CARPENTER SHOP. IN THE EVENINGS WHEN THE DAY'S WORK IS DONE, THEY REST ON THE ROOF TOP--WATCHING THE STARS AND TALKING ABOUT GOD'S PROMISE TO MARY.

BUT ONE DAY JOSEPH COMES HOME FROM THE MARKET PLACE WITH BAD NEWS: CAESAR AUGUSTUS HAS ORDERED EVERYONE TO REGISTER HIS NAME AND PROPERTY. SINCE JOSEPH AND MARY ARE DESCENDANTS OF KING DAVID, JOSEPH MUST GO TO BETHLEHEM, THE CITY OF DAVID.

BUT I CAN'T GO NOW-- AND LEAVE YOU...

YOU MUST GO, JOSEPH, AND I'LL GO WITH YOU. DON'T WORRY-- GOD WILL BE WITH US.

EAGER TO HAVE THE REGISTRATION OVER, THEY SET OUT. SOON OTHERS JOIN THEM ON THE WAY. BUT THE JOURNEY TAKES SEVERAL DAYS, AND AFTER A WHILE JOSEPH AND MARY FALL BEHIND-- UNTIL THEY ARE AMONG THE LAST TO REACH BETHLEHEM.

WE HAVE TRAVELED A LONG WAY AND MY WIFE IS VERY TIRED. I NEED A ROOM.

I'M SORRY, BUT BETHLEHEM IS CROWDED THESE DAYS. THERE'S NO ROOM HERE.

153

THAT SAME NIGHT SOME SHEPHERDS ARE WATCHING THEIR SHEEP ON THE HILLS OUTSIDE THE CITY. THEY TALK OF THE CROWDS THAT HAVE COME TO BETHLEHEM.

SUDDENLY-- A GREAT LIGHT SHINES AROUND THE SHEPHERDS.

I'VE HEARD THAT CAESAR AUGUSTUS ORDERED THIS REGISTRATION SO THAT HE CAN COLLECT MORE TAXES. WILL WE NEVER BE FREE FROM THESE FOREIGN TYRANTS?

GOD HAS PROMISED US A DELIVERER. AND ALL MY LIFE I HAVE PRAYED THAT I WOULD LIVE TO SEE HIM.

WHAT IS IT?

O GOD, PROTECT US.

FEAR NOT; FOR I BRING YOU GOOD NEWS OF GREAT JOY FOR ALL THE PEOPLE. FOR TO YOU IS BORN IN THE CITY OF DAVID A SAVIOR, WHO IS CHRIST THE LORD. YOU WILL FIND THE BABY LYING IN A MANGER.

THEN THE SKY IS FILLED WITH A GREAT CHOIR OF ANGELS -- SINGING THEIR PRAISE TO GOD.

Glory to God in the highest, and on earth peace, good will toward men.

THE ANGELS LEAVE -- THE BEAUTIFUL LIGHT DISAPPEARS. ONCE AGAIN IT IS DARK AND STILL ON THE BETHLEHEM HILLS.

I CAN SCARCELY BELIEVE WHAT I HAVE SEEN AND HEARD. GOD HAS SENT OUR DELIVERER, OUR SAVIOR -- **TONIGHT!**

AND TO THINK HE SENT HIS ANGEL TO TELL POOR SHEPHERDS LIKE US!

THE ANGEL SAID WE WOULD FIND THE SAVIOR IN A MANGER. LET'S GO TO BETHLEHEM AND SEE HIM.

EAGERLY -- AND WITH AWE AND WONDER -- THE SHEPHERDS HURRY TO BETHLEHEM. INSIDE THE GATE THEY TURN TOWARD THE INN...

LOOK -- THERE'S A LIGHT IN THE STABLE!

OUR SAVIOR IS HERE! AND I'M GOING TO SEE HIM!

...AND GO BACK TO THEIR FLOCKS, STILL PRAISING GOD FOR WHAT HAS HAPPENED THAT NIGHT. AT THE SAME TIME IN A LAND FAR TO THE EAST, WISE MEN TALK ABOUT A STRANGE THING THEY HAVE JUST SEEN.

THAT NEW STAR-- IT'S BRIGHTER THAN ALL THE REST. IT MUST HAVE A SPECIAL MEANING.

IT IS A SIGN FROM GOD THAT THE GREAT KING OF THE JEWS HAS BEEN BORN.

LET US GO TO JERUSALEM AND FIND THE KING.

AFTER MONTHS OF TRAVEL, THE WISE MEN REACH JERUSALEM.

WE HAVE COME TO WORSHIP THE ONE BORN TO BE KING OF THE JEWS. PLEASE TELL US WHERE WE CAN FIND HIM.

YOU MUST BE MISTAKEN. NO KING HAS BEEN BORN HERE RECENTLY.

WHEN THE WISE MEN INQUIRE AT THE PALACE, KING HEROD-- WHO HAS COMMITTED MORE THAN ONE MURDER TO PROTECT HIS THRONE-- IS FRIGHTENED. HE CALLS FOR THE CHIEF PRIESTS AND SCRIBES.

IS THERE ANYTHING IN THE SACRED BOOKS TELLING ABOUT A BABY WHO WILL BECOME KING OF THE JEWS?

YES, THE SCRIPTURES SAY HE WILL BE BORN IN BETHLEHEM.

SECRETLY HEROD SENDS FOR THE WISE MEN AND ASKS THEM WHEN THEY SAW THE STAR AND HOW LONG IT TOOK THEM TO COME TO JERUSALEM. THEN HE SPEAKS VERY SLYLY.

LOOK FOR THE CHILD IN BETHLEHEM. WHEN YOU FIND HIM, COME BACK AND TELL ME WHERE HE IS SO THAT I MAY WORSHIP HIM, TOO.

AND WHEN I FIND THAT CHILD, I'LL KILL HIM. NO ONE IS GOING TO BE KING OF THE JEWS BUT ME!

157

FOLLOWING HEROD'S INSTRUCTIONS, THE WISE MEN SET OUT FOR BETHLEHEM. AS THEY LEAVE JERUSALEM, THEY AGAIN SEE THE STAR THEY HAD SEEN IN THE EAST. IT LEADS THEM TO BETHLEHEM, AND THERE...

LOOK! THE STAR HAS STOPPED ABOVE THAT HOUSE!

OUR JOURNEY IS FINISHED! SOON WE'LL SEE THE CHILD WHO IS TO BE KING OF THE JEWS!

PEOPLE IN BETHLEHEM ARE SURPRISED TO SEE THE IMPORTANT-LOOKING STRANGERS STOP BEFORE THE HOUSE WHERE JOSEPH AND MARY NOW LIVE. WHEN THE WISE MEN TELL THEIR REASON FOR COMING, THEY ARE INVITED INSIDE. THERE THEY KNEEL BEFORE THE BABY JESUS.

WE HAVE COME A LONG WAY TO WORSHIP THE ROYAL CHILD.

AND TO BRING HIM GIFTS OF GOLD, FRANKINCENSE, AND MYRRH.

THAT NIGHT AT THE INN THE WISE
MEN MAKE PLANS FOR THEIR
RETURN HOME.

I'M GLAD THAT WE CAN GO BACK TO JERUSALEM AND TELL KING HEROD WHERE HE CAN FIND THE BABY.

THE NEXT MORNING...

I HAD A DREAM—

SO DID I! IN MY DREAM GOD WARNED US NOT TO RETURN TO JERUSALEM BECAUSE HEROD IS JEALOUS AND WANTS TO KILL THE CHILD.

I HAD THE SAME DREAM! HEROD WILL FIND OUT NOTHING FROM US. WE'LL GO HOME BY ANOTHER ROUTE.

159

BUT THE WISE MEN ARE NOT THE ONLY ONES WHO ARE WARNED OF HEROD'S ANGER. AN ANGEL OF GOD APPEARS TO JOSEPH, TOO...

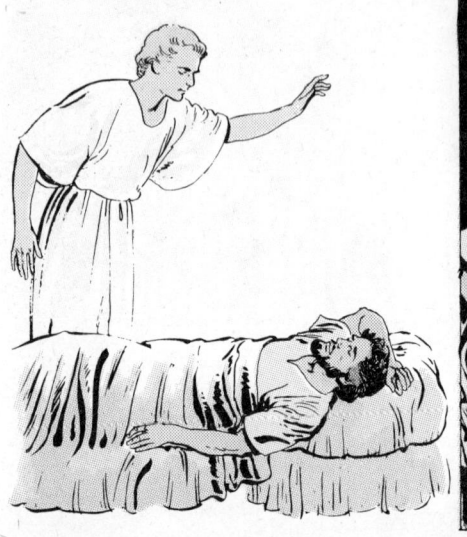

MARY! AN ANGEL HAS TOLD ME WE MUST ESCAPE AT ONCE -- TO EGYPT. HEROD WANTS TO KILL JESUS.

KILL JESUS OH, NO

IN THE MIDDLE OF THE NIGHT, JOSEPH AND MARY WITH THE BABY JESUS STEAL QUIETLY OUT OF THE CITY.

IN JERUSALEM, HEROD WAITS FOR THE RETURN OF THE WISE MEN WHEN THEY DO NOT COME, HE SUSPECTS THEY ARE TRYING TO PROTE THE CHILD -- FROM HIM.

THAT CHILD WILL NEVER LIVE TO TAKE **MY** THRONE I'LL KILL EVERY BABY IN BETHLEHEM BEFORE I LET HIM ESCAPE.

Temptation
in the
Desert

AS SOON AS JOHN, THE COUSIN OF JESUS, IS OLD ENOUGH TO UNDERSTAND, HIS FATHER TELLS HIM: "BEFORE YOU WERE BORN, GOD PLANNED FOR YOU TO SERVE HIM IN A SPECIAL WAY." JOHN GROWS UP PREPARING TO SERVE GOD. AND AFTER THE DEATH OF HIS PARENTS HE GOES INTO THE WILDERNESS TO PRAY AND STUDY. THERE GOD CALLS HIM TO BEGIN HIS WORK.

O GOD, I'M READY TO PREPARE THE WAY FOR THE COMING OF THE SAVIOR.

JOHN PUTS HIS WORDS INTO ACTION AND BEGINS PREACHING ALONG THE JORDAN RIVER.

REPENT OF YOUR SINS AND BE BAPTIZED, FOR GOD'S KINGDOM IS CLOSE AT HAND.

NEWS SPREADS FAR AND WIDE ABOUT THE MAN WHO LOOKS AND SPEAKS LIKE A PROPHET OF OLD. CROWDS COME OUT FROM JERUSALEM TO HEAR THE MAN CALLED JOHN THE BAPTIST. SOME ARE ONLY CURIOUS, BUT JOHN KNOWS THEIR THOUGHTS.

DO YOU THINK THAT JUST BECAUSE YOU ARE JEWS YOU WILL BE ALLOWED IN GOD'S KINGDOM? NO, YOU MUST REPENT--

THE SCOFFERS TURN AWAY, BUT MANY PEOPLE LISTEN EAGERLY. ONE DAY A CROWD GATHERS AT THE JORDAN RIVER.

ARE YOU THE SAVIOR GOD HAS PROMISED US?

NO. I BAPTIZE WITH WATER, BUT HE WILL BAPTIZE WITH THE HOLY SPIRIT OF GOD. PREPARE YOURSELVES; THE SAVIOR IS COMING!

UNKNOWN TO JOHN, THE VERY ONE HE IS TALKING ABOUT IS IN THE CROWD. JESUS HAS COME DOWN FROM NAZARETH TO HEAR HIM. HE ASKS TO BE BAPTIZED.

WHY DO YOU COME TO **ME** FOR BAPTISM? IT IS **I** WHO NEED TO BE BAPTIZED BY YOU.

IT IS GOOD, JOHN, FOR US TO SHOW THAT WE BELONG TO GOD'S KINGDOM.

So JOHN BAPTIZES JESUS. AND WHEN JESUS COMES UP OUT OF THE WATER, THE SPIRIT OF GOD DESCENDS LIKE A DOVE UPON HIM. THEN A VOICE FROM HEAVEN SPEAKS:

THIS IS MY BELOVED SON IN WHOM I AM WELL PLEASED.

THE CROWDS DO NOT UNDERSTAND WHAT HAS HAPPENED-- THEY GO HOME, NOT REALIZING THAT THEY HAVE SEEN THEIR SAVIOR. JOHN CONTINUES PREACHING -- REPENT OF YOUR SINS, FOR THE KINGDOM OF GOD IS COMING SOON.

To JESUS, THE WORDS OF HIS FATHER ARE A SIGN OF APPROVAL, AND THE GIFT OF THE HOLY SPIRIT IS AN ASSURANCE OF HELP FOR THE WORK GOD HAS SENT HIM TO DO. HE GOES INTO THE WILDERNESS -- ALONE -- TO THINK ABOUT HIS PLAN FOR ESTABLISHING GOD'S KINGDOM.

At THE END OF FORTY DAYS, JESUS IS HUNGRY. AS HE THINKS OF FOOD, HE HEARS THE VOICE OF THE DEVIL TEMPTING HIM TO USE HIS DIVINE POWER FOR HIS OWN BENEFIT. "IF YOU ARE REALLY THE SON OF GOD," THE DEVIL SAYS, "TURN THIS STONE INTO BREAD. AFTER ALL, GOD WOULD NOT WANT HIS BELOVED SON TO BE HUNGRY."

SCRIPTURE SAYS, "MAN SHALL NOT LIVE BY BREAD ALONE, BUT BY THE WORD OF GOD."

THE DEVIL DOESN'T GIVE UP EASILY. HE TRIES AGAIN-- AND THIS TIME WITH A MORE POWERFUL TEMPTATION ...

166

TO PREVENT JESUS FROM CARRYING OUT GOD'S WORK, THE DEVIL TEMPTS HIM TO SEEK EARTHLY POWERS FOR HIMSELF. BUT JESUS REFUSES. THE DEVIL TRIES AGAIN--THIS TIME HE TEMPTS JESUS TO MAKE HIMSELF POPULAR BY DOING SOMETHING SENSATIONAL.

"LET PEOPLE SEE YOUR DIVINE POWER BY THROWING YOURSELF FROM THE ROOF OF THE TEMPLE," THE DEVIL SAYS. "FOR, IF YOU ARE THE SON OF GOD, HIS ANGELS WILL TAKE CARE OF YOU."

THE SCRIPTURES SAY, "THOU SHALT NOT TEMPT GOD."

HAVING REJECTED EVERY TEMPTATION, JESUS LEAVES THE WILDERNESS AND GOES BACK TO BETHANY BEYOND THE JORDAN.

Jesus'
Miracles

AS JESUS ENTERS BETHANY, JOHN THE BAPTIST POINTS HIM OUT TO TWO OF HIS OWN DISCIPLES --ANDREW AND JOHN.

THERE IS THE SAVIOR I HAVE BEEN TELLING YOU ABOUT.

THE TWO MEN TURN AND QUICKLY FOLLOW JESUS.

MASTER-- MAY WE TALK WITH YOU?

YES, COME WITH ME TO MY LODGING PLACE.

LISTENING TO JESUS IS SUCH A WON-DERFUL EXPERIENCE THAT HOURS GO BY BEFORE ANDREW SUDDENLY REMEMBERS...

MY BROTHER! HE CAME DOWN HERE FROM CAPERNAUM WITH ME TO HEAR JOHN THE BAPTIST. I MUST FIND HIM AND BRING HIM TO SEE YOU.

ANDREW RUNS TO THE HOUSE WHERE HE AND HIS BROTHER ARE STAYING.

SIMON! I HAVE FOUND THE SAVIOR!

170

SIMON EAGERLY FOLLOWS ANDREW BACK THROUGH THE WINDING STREETS OF BETHANY.

THIS IS SIMON, MY BROTHER.

YES, YOU ARE SIMON, BUT FROM NOW ON YOU SHALL BE CALLED PETER, BECAUSE YOU WILL BE LIKE A ROCK.

THE NEXT DAY JESUS GOES NORTH TO GALILEE. HE INVITES ANOTHER YOUNG MAN, PHILIP, TO BE HIS DISCIPLE AND GO WITH HIM.

PHILIP ACCEPTS JESUS' INVITATION. LIKE ANDREW, HE WANTS TO SHARE HIS GOOD NEWS, SO HE HURRIES TO TELL A FRIEND.

NATHANAEL--COME WITH ME! I HAVE FOUND THE SAVIOR! HE IS JESUS OF NAZARETH.

NAZARETH? CAN ANYTHING GOOD COME FROM **THAT** TOWN?

IF WHAT YOU SAY IS TRUE, MEN WOULD GIVE UP EVERYTHING THEY HAVE TO FOLLOW HIM.

COME AND SEE FOR YOURSELF!

NATHANAEL SEES JESUS, BUT HE STILL DOESN'T BELIEVE. THEN JESUS SPEAKS...

171

PHILIP IS SO EXCITED ABOUT SEEING JESUS THAT HE HURRIES TO TELL A FRIEND. "NATHANAEL, COME WITH ME. I HAVE FOUND THE SAVIOR!" NATHANAEL DOUBTS SUCH NEWS, BUT HE AGREES TO SEE FOR HIMSELF. AS THEY APPROACH JESUS...

BEHOLD, A MAN IN WHOM THERE IS NOTHING DECEITFUL.

HOW DO **YOU** KNOW ANYTHING ABOUT ME?

BEFORE PHILIP CALLED YOU, YOU WERE SITTING UNDER A FIG TREE THINKING ABOUT GOD. I SAW YOU THERE.

YOU **ARE** THE SAVIOR FOR WHOM WE HAVE WAITED SO LONG!

HAVING FOUND HIS SAVIOR, NATHANAEL FORGETS EVERY-THING ELSE AND JOINS JESUS AND HIS FRIENDS AS THEY TRAVEL NORTH TO GALILEE. AT THE CROSSROADS, PETER AND ANDREW TURN OFF TO THEIR HOME NEAR THE SEA OF GALILEE; THE OTHERS GO ON TO CANA.

172

WHEN THEY REACH THE TOWN THEY ARE GREETED BY A FRIEND OF JESUS.

PLEASE COME TO MY WEDDING FEAST -- YOUR MOTHER WILL BE THERE.

THANK YOU-- WE WOULD LIKE TO SHARE YOUR HAPPINESS.

DURING THE FEAST MARY DISCOVERS SOMETHING THAT WILL EMBARRASS THE GROOM -- THERE IS NO MORE WINE. SHE TELLS JESUS, THEN SHE GOES TO THE SERVANTS.

DO WHATEVER HE TELLS YOU.

FILL THESE JARS WITH WATER.

WHY WATER? IT'S WINE WE NEED.

BUT THE SERVANTS SENSE A STRANGE AUTHORITY IN JESUS, AND THEY OBEY HIM.

NOW TAKE SOME TO THE HEADWAITER.

WHY -- IT **IS** WINE! IT'S A MIRACLE!

THIS MAN MUST BE A PROPHET OF GOD -- NO ORDINARY MAN COULD DO SUCH A THING!

THE HEADWAITER IS SO SURPRISED WHEN HE TASTES THE WINE THAT HE CALLS THE GROOM AWAY FROM THE FEAST.

SIR, THE BEST WINE IS USUALLY SERVED FIRST. BUT YOU HAVE SAVED THE BEST TO THE LAST.

I'M GLAD IF PEOPLE ARE HAPPY.

WHEN JESUS' DISCIPLES HEAR ABOUT THE MIRACLE, THEY TOO ARE EXCITED. THEY TALK ABOUT IT AS THEY GO DOWN TO JERUSALEM WITH JESUS FOR THE PASSOVER FEAST. THE CITY IS CROWDED WITH PEOPLE WHO HAVE HEARD JOHN THE BAPTIST TELL ABOUT THE COMING OF THE MESSIAH. "HOW WILL WE RECOGNIZE HIM?" THEY ASK.

AS JESUS WALKS THROUGH THE BUSY STREETS, HE HEALS THE LAME AND THE SICK.

I CAN WALK! PRAISE BE TO GOD--THIS MAN HEALED ME!

BECAUSE OF THESE MIRACLES, PEOPLE BEG TO ASK: "IS JESUS THE MESSIAH?" ONE NIGH AFTER THE STREETS ARE EMPTY, A JUDGE C THE JEWIS SUPREME COURT STEALS THROUGH THE STRE OF JERU SALEM C A SECRE MISSION

175

YOU WERE BORN ONCE OF EARTHLY PARENTS. BUT YOU MUST BE BORN AGAIN OF GOD'S SPIRIT TO LIVE IN GOD'S KINGDOM.

I DON'T UNDERSTAND.

YOU CAN'T SEE THE WIND, BUT YOU CAN SEE WHAT IT DOES. YOU CANNOT SEE THE SPIRIT OF GOD, BUT YOU CAN TELL BY THE WAY A MAN LIVES IF HE HAS BEEN BORN AGAIN AND HAS THE SPIRIT OF GOD IN HIS HEART. GOD LOVES THE WORLD, AND HE HAS SENT ME TO GIVE THIS NEW LIFE TO ALL WHO BELIEVE IN ME.

NICODEMUS GOES AWAY--STILL PUZZLED, BUT WANTING TO LEARN MORE ABOUT JESUS AND HIS TEACHINGS.

JESUS SEES THAT MANY OF THE PEOPLE IN JERUSALEM ARE NOT READY TO RECEIVE HIM AS THEIR SAVIOR, SO HE LEAVES THE CITY. IN JUDEA HE TELLS THE PEOPLE ABOUT GOD'S KINGDOM AND WHAT THEY MUST DO TO ENTER IT. HERE, THE PEOPLE LISTEN EAGERLY.

THIS TEACHER IS GREATER THAN ALL THE PROPHETS.

NEWS OF JESUS' SUCCESSFUL MINISTRY IN JUDEA REACHES JOHN THE BAPTIST.

I'VE HEARD THAT JESUS IS BECOMING MORE POPULAR EVERY DAY.

THANK GOD, I HAVE FULFILLED MY MISSION OF PREPARING THE WAY FOR HIM. JESUS' INFLUENCE MUST INCREASE, AND MINE DECREASE.

Through the Roof

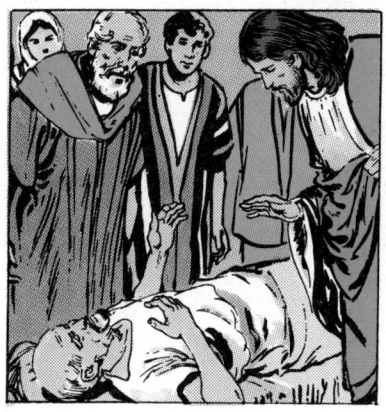

THE PEOPLE ARE AMAZED, BUT THE PHARISEES,* WHO HAVE COME OUT OF CURIOSITY TO HEAR JESUS, ARE ANGRY.

WHO IS THIS MAN WHO PRETENDS TO FORGIVE SINS?

HOW DARE HE ACT AS IF HE IS GOD!

*The Pharisees are a group of Jews who believe in obeying not only the laws God gave to Moses but the hundreds of rules they have made--such as how far a man can walk on the Sabbath. Because Jesus is more concerned about helping people than obeying their rules, the Pharisees turn against him.

JESUS KNOWS WHAT THE PHARISEES ARE THINKING.

WHICH IS EASIER-- TO SAY TO THE SICK, "YOUR SINS ARE FORGIVEN," OR TO SAY, "ARISE, TAKE UP YOUR BED, AND WALK"?

BUT SO THAT ALL MAY KNOW THAT I HAVE DIVINE POWER TO DO BOTH, I SAY TO YOU, "ARISE, TAKE UP YOUR BED, AND GO TO YOUR HOME."

MY SINS ARE FORGIVEN! I'M HEALED! GLORY BE TO GOD!

I'VE NEVER SEEN ANYTHING LIKE IT.

NEITHER HAVE I. BUT IF HE IS TRYING TO MAKE US THINK HE IS THE MESSIAH, WHY DOESN'T HE DO SOMETHING ABOUT OVERTHROWING THE ROMANS?

JESUS LEAVES THE HOUSE WHERE HE HAS BEEN TEACHING, AND AS HE PASSES BY THE TOLL HOUSE AT THE CITY GATE...

YOU TAX COLLECTORS ARE ALL ROBBERS. I CAN'T PAY THAT MUCH TAX, AND YOU KNOW IT.

YOU'D BETTER PAY IT! REMEMBER — I HAVE THE POWER OF THE WHOLE ROMAN EMPIRE BEHIND ME.

IN ALL CAPERNAUM THERE IS
NO JEW MORE DESPISED THAN
MATTHEW, A TAX COLLECTOR
FOR ROME. ONE DAY AS HE AND
A MERCHANT ARE ARGUING
ABOUT TAXES ON A CARAVAN
OF GOODS, JESUS PASSES
BY. HE LOOKS STRAIGHT INTO
THE EYES OF THE HATED
TAX COLLECTOR...

MATTHEW, FOLLOW ME.

181

TO THE AMAZEMENT OF THE CROWD, MATTHEW TURNS FROM HIS WORK AND FOLLOWS JESUS.

I CAN'T BELIEVE IT! MATTHEW IS GIVING UP HIS JOB TO GO WITH A MAN OF GOD!

STRANGE -- NO GOOD JEW EVER WANTED MATTHEW FOR A FRIEND.

MATTHEW IS SO HAPPY TO START A NEW LIFE WITH JESUS THAT HE GIVES A BIG FEAST AND INVITES HIS FRIENDS TO MEET JESUS. SOME PHARISEES WHO ARE PASSING BY LOOK ON -- SURPRISED.

WHY DOES YOUR MASTER EAT WITH ALL THOSE SINNERS?

JESUS ANSWERS FOR HIS DISCIPLE.

ONLY THE SICK NEED A DOCTOR. I HAVE COME NOT TO CALL THE RIGHTEOUS BUT SINNERS TO REPENT.

THE PHARISEES HAVE NO ANSWER TO THIS -- BUT IT MAKES THEM EVEN MORE ANGRY. SO EVERYWHERE JESUS GOES THEY WATCH FOR A CHANCE TO CRITICIZE HIM. ONE SABBATH DAY IN THE SYNAGOGUE...

LOOK -- JESUS IS TALKING TO THAT MAN WITH THE WITHERED HAND. LET'S SEE IF WE CAN CATCH HIM BREAKING A SABBATH LAW. THEN WE'LL HAVE A CASE AGAINST HIM.

Betrayed!

IT IS THE FIRST DAY OF THE WEEK. THE ROAD TO JERUSALEM IS FILLED WITH PEOPLE ON THE WAY TO CELEBRATE THE PASSOVER FEAST OF THE JEWS. AT JESUS' REQUEST HIS DISCIPLES BRING HIM A LOWLY BEAST OF BURDEN -- HE MOUNTS IT AND JOINS THE MULTITUDE OF PILGRIMS. EAGERLY THEY MAKE WAY FOR HIM -- WAVING PALM BRANCHES AND CARPETING HIS PATH WITH THEIR GARMENTS. AND, WHILE THEY ESCORT HIM -- TRIUMPHANTLY -- UP THE ROAD AND INTO THE CITY, THE SOUND OF THEIR PRAISES FILLS THE AIR: "HOSANNA! BLESSED IS THE KING THAT COMETH IN THE NAME OF THE LORD!"

DURING ITS LONG HISTORY JERUSALEM HAS SEEN MANY PROCESSIONS ENTER ITS GATES-- KINGS ON HORSEBACK AND CONQUERORS WITH ARMED LEGIONS-- BUT NEVER ONE LIKE THIS.

WHO IS THIS MAN?

JESUS, THE PROPHET OF NAZARETH!

BUT THE NEWS THAT JESUS IS COMING HAS ALREADY SPREAD THROUGH THE CITY. WHEN HE REACHES THE TEMPLE, HE FINDS THE BLIND, LAME, AND SICK THERE WAITING.

RISE UP, MY CHILD, AND WALK.

HOSANNA TO THE SON OF DAVID!

THE CHILDREN'S PRAISE ANGERS THE PRIESTS AND PHARISEES.

DO YOU HEAR WHAT THEY ARE SAYING?

YES, AND HAVE YOU NOT READ IN THE PSALMS THAT OUT OF THE MOUTHS OF CHILDREN GOD BRINGS PERFECT PRAISE?

THAT EVENING JESUS GOES BACK TO BETHANY, BUT ON MONDAY WHEN HE RETURNS TO THE TEMPLE IN JERUSALEM...

I HAVE COME A LONG WAY TO OFFER A SACRIFICE TO GOD, BUT I CAN'T PAY SUCH A HIGH PRICE FOR THE DOVES.

SOMEONE ELSE WILL-- SO MOVE ON.

IN RIGHTEOUS ANGER JESUS DRIVES THE MERCHANTS OUT OF THE TEMPLE.

IS IT NOT WRITTEN IN THE SCRIPTURES THAT "MY HOUSE SHALL BE CALLED A HOUSE OF PRAYER"? BUT YOU HAVE MADE IT A DEN OF THIEVES.

WHEN JESUS BEGINS TO PREACH, PEOPLE CROWD INTO THE TEMPLE COURTS TO HEAR HIM. BUT BEHIND CLOSED DOORS THE PRIESTS AND PHARISEES PLOT THEIR STRATEGY. BY TUESDAY THEY ARE READY...

MASTER, WE KNOW YOU TEACH THE TRUTH. TELL US, IS IT RIGHT TO PAY TAXES TO CAESAR, OR NOT?

IF HE SAYS "YES," THE PEOPLE WILL TURN AGAINST HIM BECAUSE THEY HATE TO PAY TAXES TO ROME; IF HE SAYS "NO," ROME WILL ARREST HIM FOR TREASON.

HE'S TRAPPED THIS TIME FOR SURE!

GIVE TO CAESAR THE THINGS THAT ARE HIS, AND TO GOD THE THINGS THAT ARE GOD'S.

THE PHARISEES ARE ANGRY AT BEING DEFEATED AGAIN, BUT THEY MARVEL AT JESUS' SKILL IN HANDLING THEIR TRICK QUESTION. LATER IN THE DAY ONE OF THEM ASKS ANOTHER DIFFICULT QUESTION.

WHICH OF OUR 613 COMMANDMENTS IS THE MOST IMPORTANT?

.THOU SHALT LOVE THE LORD THY GOD WITH ALL THY HEART, AND WITH ALL THY SOUL, AND WITH ALL THY MIND, AND WITH ALL THY STRENGTH. AND THE SECOND IS THIS: THOU SHALT LOVE THY NEIGHBOR AS THYSELF.

YOU HAVE SPOKEN THE TRUTH. TO LOVE GOD AND ONE'S NEIGHBOR IS MORE IMPORTANT THAN ALL BURNT OFFERINGS.

YOU ARE NOT FAR FROM THE KINGDOM OF GOD.

190

Later that week, Jesus and his disciples come together for the Passover meal in an upstairs room they have prepared.

IF I, YOUR LORD AND MASTER, HAVE SERVED YOU, YOU SHOULD DO THE SAME FOR ONE ANOTHER. THE SERVANT IS NOT GREATER THAN HIS MASTER.

AFTER A FEW MINUTES JESUS MAKES STARTLING STATEMENT.

ONE OF YOU IS GOING TO BETRAY ME.

BETRAY YOU? IS IT I, LORD?

JESUS REPLIES THAT IT IS ONE WHO IS EATING WITH HIM NOW. JUDAS LEANS FORWARD.

IS IT I?

YOU HAVE SAID IT. WHAT YOU ARE GOING TO DO, JUDAS, DO QUICKLY.

AT ONCE THE TRAITOR RISES FROM THE TABLE AND HURRIES AWAY. BUT THE OTHER DISCIPLES DO NOT UNDERSTAND WH

AFTER JUDAS, THE TRAITOR, LEAVES, JESUS PICKS UP A PIECE OF BREAD, THANKS GOD FOR IT, BREAKS IT, AND GIVES IT TO HIS DISCIPLES, SAYING, "THIS IS MY BODY." WHEN THEY HAVE EATEN THE BREAD, HE OFFERS THEM A CUP.

DRINK OF IT, EACH ONE OF YOU, FOR IT IS MY BLOOD, WHICH WILL BE SHED TO PAY THE PRICE OF YOUR SINS. AFTER I'M GONE, DO THIS IN REMEMBRANCE OF ME.

THUS JESUS MAKES A NEW COVENANT BETWEEN GOD AND MEN. AS MEN TAKE THE BREAD AND WINE IN THE NAME OF JESUS THEY ARE REMINDED THAT GOD, THROUGH HIS SON, HAS DELIVERED THEM FROM THE SLAVERY OF SIN.

IN A LITTLE WHILE I MUST LEAVE YOU. YOU CANNOT FOLLOW ME, BUT BEFORE I GO, LET ME REMIND YOU: LOVE ONE ANOTHER AS I HAVE LOVED YOU.

LORD, WHY CAN'T I FOLLOW YOU? YOU KNOW I'D GIVE MY LIFE FOR YOU.

PETER, BEFORE THE COCK CROWS YOU WILL DENY ME THREE TIMES.

DENY MY LORD? NEVER! MY SWORD IS READY THIS MINUTE FOR THE FIRST PERSON WHO TRIES TO HARM HIM.

THE DISCIPLES ARE FRIGHTENED AT THE THOUGHT OF JESUS LEAVING THEM.

DO NOT BE AFRAID. BELIEVE IN GOD; BELIEVE ALSO IN ME. IF YOU LOVE ME, KEEP MY COMMANDMENTS. AND I WILL ASK GOD TO SEND YOU THE HOLY SPIRIT TO COMFORT YOU. HE WILL BE WITH YOU FOREVER. COME, IT IS TIME TO GO...

QUIETLY, THEY LEAVE THE UPPER ROOM. THEY WALK THROUGH THE MOONLIT STREETS OF THE CITY, OUT AN EAST GATE, AND ACROSS A VALLEY TO THE GARDEN OF GETHSEMANE ON THE MOUNT OF OLIVES.

AT THE ENTRANCE JESUS ASKS EIGHT OF THE DISCIPLES TO WAIT WHILE HE TAKES HIS CLOSEST DISCIPLES, PETER, JAMES, AND JOHN FARTHER INTO THE GARDEN.

THIS IS A SAD NIGHT FOR ME -- STAY HERE AND WATCH WHILE I GO ALONE TO PRAY.

O MY FATHER, IF THOU BE WILLING, REMOVE THIS AGONY FROM ME; NEVERTHELESS, NOT MY WILL, BUT THINE BE DONE.

WHEN JESUS RETURNS TO HIS DISCIPLES, HE FINDS THEM SLEEPING. TWO MORE TIMES HE GOES ASIDE TO PRAY, AND EACH TIME HE FINDS HIS FRIENDS ASLEEP. AFTER WAKING THEM THE THIRD TIME...

ARISE -- THE ONE WHO IS TO BETRAY ME IS NEAR.

195

AS JESUS SPEAKS, JUDAS LEADS A BAND OF MEN INTO THE GARDEN. ACCORDING TO HIS AGREEMENT, HE IDENTIFIES JESUS WITH A KISS.

GREETINGS, MASTER!

AS THE SOLDIERS TAKE HOLD OF JESUS, PETER DRAWS HIS SWORD. SLASHING WILDLY, HE CUTS OFF THE EAR OF A SERVANT.

PETER, PUT UP YOUR SWORD. DO YOU THINK THAT I CANNOT CALL ON GOD TO SEND LEGIONS OF ANGELS TO PROTECT ME?

QUIETLY JESUS HEALS THE MAN'S EAR. WHEN THE DISCIPLES SEE THAT JESUS IS MAKING NO ATTEMPT TO SAVE HIMSELF, THEY RUN FOR THEIR LIVES. AT AN OFFICER'S COMMAND, THE SOLDIERS BIND JESUS AND TAKE HIM BACK TO JERUSALEM -- THE CITY INTO WHICH HE HAD RIDDEN SO TRIUMPHANTLY ONLY A FEW DAYS BEFORE!

Condemned
to Die

198

WHILE JESUS IS SUFFERING THESE INSULTS, PETER -- WHO HAS SECRETLY FOLLOWED HIM INTO THE CITY -- WARMS HIS HANDS BY A FIRE IN THE PALACE COURTYARD. WHILE HE IS TALKING, A MAID STOPS AND LOOKS AT HIM...

YOU WERE ONE OF THOSE WITH JESUS OF NAZARETH.

ME? I DON'T KNOW WHAT YOU'RE TALKING ABOUT.

AFRAID OF BEING QUESTIONED FURTHER, PETER GOES OUT INTO THE HALLWAY, BUT THERE...

THIS FELLOW WAS WITH JESUS.

JESUS? I DON'T EVEN KNOW THE MAN.

ABOUT AN HOUR LATER SOME MEN APPROACH PETER.

DIDN'T I SEE YOU IN THE GARDEN WHEN THE SOLDIERS TOOK JESUS?

YOU ARE A GALILEAN LIKE JESUS. I CAN TELL BY THE WAY YOU TALK.

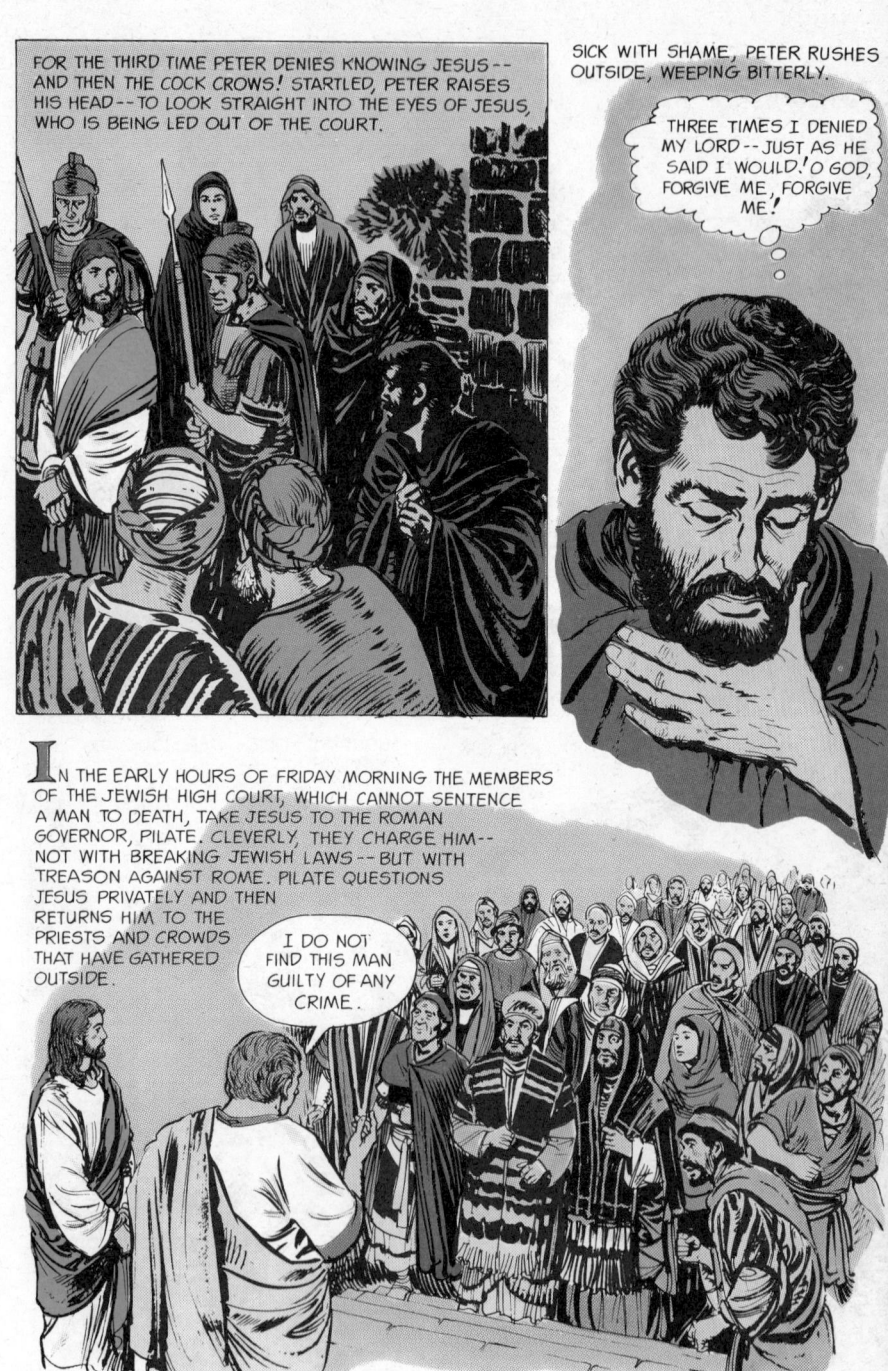

FOR THE THIRD TIME PETER DENIES KNOWING JESUS-- AND THEN THE *COCK CROWS!* STARTLED, PETER RAISES HIS HEAD--TO LOOK STRAIGHT INTO THE EYES OF JESUS, WHO IS BEING LED OUT OF THE COURT.

SICK WITH SHAME, PETER RUSHES OUTSIDE, WEEPING BITTERLY.

THREE TIMES I DENIED MY LORD--JUST AS HE SAID I WOULD.' O GOD, FORGIVE ME, FORGIVE ME.'

IN THE EARLY HOURS OF FRIDAY MORNING THE MEMBERS OF THE JEWISH HIGH COURT, WHICH *CANNOT SENTENCE A MAN TO DEATH,* TAKE JESUS TO THE ROMAN GOVERNOR, PILATE. CLEVERLY, THEY CHARGE HIM-- *NOT WITH BREAKING JEWISH LAWS*--BUT WITH TREASON AGAINST ROME. PILATE QUESTIONS JESUS PRIVATELY AND THEN RETURNS HIM TO THE PRIESTS AND CROWDS THAT HAVE GATHERED OUTSIDE.

I DO NOT FIND THIS MAN GUILTY OF ANY CRIME.

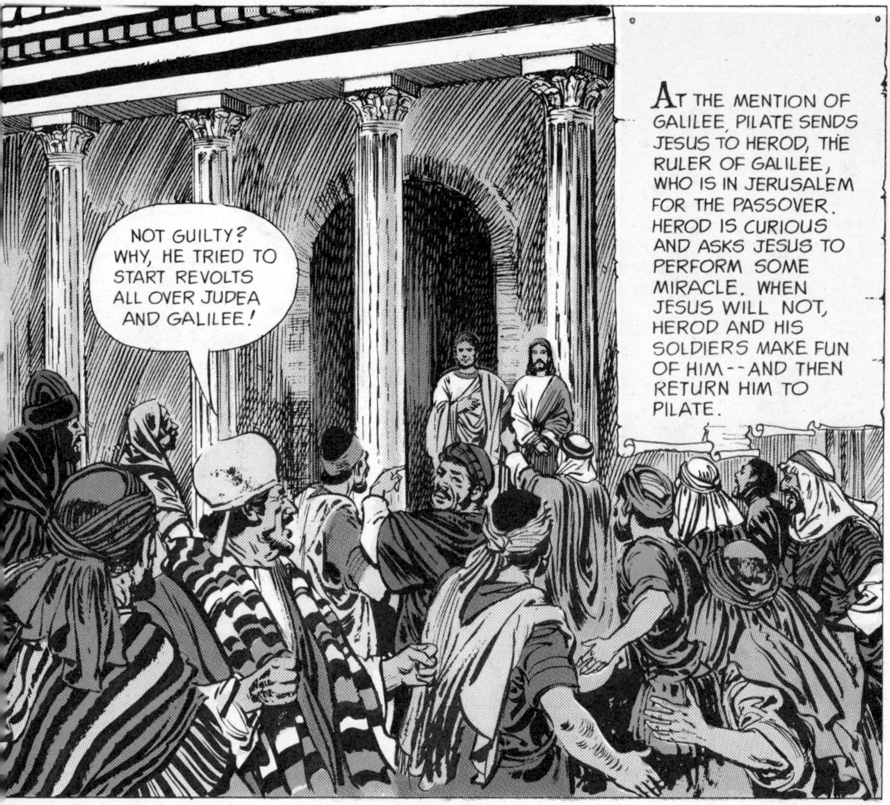

NOT GUILTY? WHY, HE TRIED TO START REVOLTS ALL OVER JUDEA AND GALILEE!

AT THE MENTION OF GALILEE, PILATE SENDS JESUS TO HEROD, THE RULER OF GALILEE, WHO IS IN JERUSALEM FOR THE PASSOVER. HEROD IS CURIOUS AND ASKS JESUS TO PERFORM SOME MIRACLE. WHEN JESUS WILL NOT, HEROD AND HIS SOLDIERS MAKE FUN OF HIM -- AND THEN RETURN HIM TO PILATE.

PILATE IS TRAPPED. HE DOES NOT BELIEVE JESUS IS GUILTY OF TREASON. "BUT, IF I LET HIM GO," HE ARGUES TO HIMSELF, "AND THE JEWISH LEADERS MAKE TROUBLE, THE EMPEROR IN ROME WILL HOLD ME RESPONSIBLE." FINALLY HE THINKS OF A WAY TO EASE HIS CONSCIENCE AND PROTECT HIMSELF...

THE PEOPLE! I'LL LET THEM DECIDE!

THE JEWISH LEADERS HAVE CHARGED JESUS WITH TREASON AGAINST ROME. PILATE, THE ROMAN GOVERNOR, DOES NOT BELIEVE HE IS GUILTY--BUT HE IS AFRAID TO ANGER THE JEWS FOR FEAR THEY WILL STIR UP SO MUCH TROUBLE THAT THE REPORTS OF IT WILL REACH THE EMPEROR IN ROME. LOOKING AT THE CROWDS IN JERUSALEM FOR THE PASSOVER, HE SUDDENLY SEES A WAY OUT: LET THE PEOPLE DECIDE WHETHER OR NOT JESUS SHOULD DIE. BUT HE DOES NOT KNOW THAT THE PRIESTS ARE STIRRING UP THE CROWDS AGAINST JESUS.

IT IS THE CUSTOM TO RELEASE A PRISONER TO YOU DURING THE PASSOVER. WHICH SHALL I GIVE YOU-- JESUS, WHO IS CALLED THE CHRIST-- OR BARABBAS, THE MURDERER?

BARABBAS! GIVE US BARABBAS!

PILATE IS STUNNED. HE MAKES ANOTHER ATTEMPT TO SAVE JESUS.

SCOURGE HIM.

MAYBE THE PEOPLE WILL BE SATISFIED IF THE PRISONER IS PUNISHED.

SO JESUS IS WHIPPED WITH LEATHER THONGS. THEN, IN SPORT, THE SOLDIERS MAKE A CROWN OF THORNS AND PLACE IT ON HIS HEAD.

HAIL, THE KING OF THE JEWS!

HOPING THE SIGHT OF JESUS, BRUTALLY BEATEN, WILL AROUSE THE CROWD'S SYMPATHY, PILATE PRESENTS HIM TO THE MULTITUDE.

BEHOLD THE MAN!

CRUCIFY HIM!

CRUCIFY HIM!

HAPPY, EXCITED PILGRIMS FROM ALL OVER PALESTINE HAVE BEEN CROWDING INTO JERUSALEM FOR DAYS TO CELEBRATE THE PASSOVER FEAST. BUT ON FRIDAY MORNING STARTLING NEWS SWEEPS ACROSS THE CITY LIKE A CHILLING WIND: JESUS OF NAZARETH IS GOING TO BE CRUCIFIED -- FOR TREASON!

THE STREET THAT LEADS TO THE HILL OF EXECUTION IS SOON FILLED WITH A STRANGE MIXTURE OF PEOPLE-- PRIESTS AND PHARISEES WHO DEMAND JESUS' DEATH; WOMEN WEEPING FOR THE MAN WHO FORGAVE SINS AND HEALED THE SICK; AND THE CURIOUS WHO WANT ONLY TO SEE A CONDEMNED MAN CARRY HIS CROSS...

IT IS ABOUT NINE O'CLOCK WHEN JESUS, AND TWO ROBBERS WHO ARE TO BE CRUCIFIED WITH HIM, REACH CALVARY. AND THERE THE SON OF GOD IS NAILED TO A CROSS. ABOVE HIS HEAD IS FASTENED A SIGN: JESUS OF NAZARETH, THE KING OF THE JEWS!

> FATHER, FORGIVE THEM: FOR THEY KNOW NOT WHAT THEY DO.

IT IS NOW NOON. SLOWLY, A STRANGE SHADOW COVERS THE LAND. FOR THREE HOURS THERE IS DARKNESS, THEN JESUS CRIES OUT TO GOD...

> FATHER, INTO THY HANDS I COMMIT MY SPIRIT.

AND HAVING DONE SO, HE DIES. THE EARTH TREMBLES, AND IN JERUSALEM...

At about nine o'clock Friday morning Jesus of Nazareth is crucified outside the walls of Jerusalem. From noon until three o'clock darkness covers the land. Then -- suddenly an earthquake rocks the ground. And in Jerusalem...

THE VEIL BEFORE THE HOLIEST PLACE IN THE TEMPLE HAS BEEN RIPPED! WHAT CAN IT MEAN?

The answer is that on a hill called Calvary the Son of God has given his life to pay for the sins of the world. The veil in the temple no longer separates man from the presence of God, for Jesus, the Son, has opened the way to God, the Father.

OUTSIDE THE CITY, EVEN THE ROMAN OFFICER WHO DIRECTED THE CRUCIFIXION IS AWED BY WHAT HAS HAPPENED. REVERENTLY, HE LOOKS UP AT THE MAN WHO FORGAVE HIS ENEMIES.

TRULY THIS MAN WAS GOD'S SON!

THE PEOPLE, TOO, ARE SHAKEN BY THE EXECUTION. AS THEY TURN BACK TO THE CITY...

I HAD HOPED THAT HE WAS THE ONE WHO WOULD DELIVER US FROM THE ROMANS.

IN JERUSALEM JOSEPH OF ARIMATHEA, A MEMBER OF THE JEWISH HIGH COURT AND SECRETLY A FOLLOWER OF JESUS, GOES BOLDLY TO PILATE.

MAY I HAVE THE BODY OF JESUS SO THAT WE MAY BURY IT BEFORE THE SABBATH?

YES... I'LL GIVE ORDERS TO MY OFFICER IN CHARGE.

207

REVERENTLY, JOSEPH TAKES THE BODY OF JESUS FROM THE CROSS. THEN HE AND HIS FRIEND, NICODEMUS, WRAP IT IN LINEN CLOTH, AND PLACE IT IN JOSEPH'S GARDEN TOMB.

EARLY THE NEXT DAY THE PRIESTS AND PHARISEES ALSO GO TO PILATE...

WE REMEMBER JESUS SAID THAT AFTER THREE DAYS HE WOULD RISE FROM THE DEAD. ORDER YOUR SOLDIERS TO SEAL AND GUARD THE TOMB SO THAT HIS DISCIPLES CAN'T STEAL THE BODY AND CLAIM THAT JESUS MADE GOOD ON HIS BOAST.

TAKE THE SOLDIERS YOU NEED AND SET UP A GUARD UNTIL AFTER THE THIRD DAY.

SO THE TOMB IS SEALED, AND ROMAN SOLDIERS ARE PLACED ON GUARD.

THERE-- THAT'S THE LAST WE'LL HEAR OF THIS MAN WHO CALLED HIMSELF THE SON OF GOD!

FRIDAY -- JUST OUTSIDE JERUSALEM -- JESUS OF NAZARETH IS CRUCIFIED AND BURIED. AT THE REQUEST OF THE PRIESTS AND PHARISEES, THE TOMB IS SEALED AND ROMAN SOLDIERS SET TO GUARD IT.

BUT ON THE MORNING OF THE THIRD DAY THE EARTH TREMBLES. AN ANGEL OF THE LORD DESCENDS -- AND ROLLS THE HEAVY STONE ASIDE. TERRIFIED, THE SOLDIERS FALL TO THE GROUND. WHEN THEY CAN GET TO THEIR FEET THEY RUSH BACK TO THE CITY.

THAT SAME MORNING MARY MAGDALENE AND OTHER FRIENDS OF JESUS HURRY TO THE TOMB WITH SPICES TO ANOINT HIS BODY. ON THE WAY, THEY WORRY ABOUT HOW THEY WILL GET THE STONE ROLLED AWAY. BUT WHEN THEY REACH THE GARDEN...

THE TOMB! IT IS OPEN!

BELIEVING THAT SOMEONE HAS STOLEN JESUS' BODY, MARY RUNS BACK TO JERUSALEM TO TELL PETER AND JOHN. BUT THE OTHERS ENTER THE TOMB -- TO FIND AN ANGEL SEATED THERE.

DON'T BE FRIGHTENED. JESUS IS RISEN. GO, TELL HIS DISCIPLES.

IN THE CITY PETER AND JOHN ARE SO STARTLED BY MARY'S NEWS THAT THEY RACE BACK AHEAD OF HER. WHEN THEY REACH THE TOMB --

ONLY HIS BURIAL CLOTHES. WHAT DO YOU MAKE OF IT?

THAT HE ROSE FROM THE DEAD -- AS HE SAID HE WOULD. OH, WHY DIDN'T WE BELIEVE HIM!

BY THE TIME MARY REACHES THE GARDEN THE OTHERS HAVE GONE. IN HER GRIEF SHE DOES NOT RECOGNIZE THE VOICE OF ONE WHO QUESTIONS HER.

WHY DO YOU WEEP?

IF YOU HAVE TAKEN JESUS' BODY, TELL ME WHERE YOU HAVE LAID IT.

SOFTLY JESUS SPEAKS HER NAME-- "MARY!" SHE TURNS--AND SEES HER RISEN LORD.

MASTER!

BUT JESUS' FRIENDS ARE NOT THE ONLY ONES WHO ARE EXCITED ABOUT WHAT HAPPENED IN THE GARDEN. IN JERUSALEM THE ROMAN SOLDIERS REPORT TO THE PRIESTS AND PHARISEES. AFRAID OF WHAT MAY HAPPEN IF THE TRUTH IS KNOWN, THEY ACT QUICKLY.

HERE, TAKE THIS MONEY. TELL PEOPLE THAT JESUS' DISCIPLES STOLE HIS BODY.

WHILE THE SOLDIERS SPREAD THEIR LIE, JESUS JOINS TWO OF HIS DISCIPLES ON THE WAY TO EMMAUS. THEY TALK WITH HIM, BUT THEY DO NOT KNOW WHO HE IS.

THAT EVENING AS THEY DINE IN EMMAUS, JESUS BLESSES THE BREAD -- AND WHEN HE HANDS IT TO THEM THEY SUDDENLY RECOGNIZE HIM.

JESUS!

AND JUST AS SUDDENLY HE VANISHES FROM THEIR SIGHT!

Within over a month Jesus appears to many of his followers. On the fortieth day he is taken to heaven. The disciples' story spreads and soon thousands of people believe in Jesus' resurrection. The group of believers grows daily.

211

Shipwrecked

Paul, a Pharisee who decided to become a follower of Jesus, preaches all over the known world and starts many churches among the non-Jewish people. However, the same kind of people who hated Jesus now hate Paul. They try to destroy Paul's ministry.

THE DAY AFTER PAUL REACHES JERUSALEM, HE MEETS WITH JAMES AND OTHER LEADERS OF THE JERUSALEM CHURCH. HE DELIVERS THE MONEY FOR THE POOR AND TELLS WHAT GOD HAS DONE IN OTHER LANDS.

I MUST WARN YOU, PAUL, YOU HAVE ENEMIES HERE WHO THINK YOU ARE A TRAITOR. EVEN THE CHRISTIAN JEWS HAVE QUESTIONS BECAUSE OF YOUR WORK AMONG THE GENTILES.

I'LL WORSHIP WITH THEM IN THE TEMPLE TO SHOW THAT I AM TRUE TO THE FAITH OF OUR FATHERS.

JAMES' WARNING COMES TRUE WITHIN THE WEEK. WHILE PAUL IS WORSHIPING IN THE TEMPLE HIS ENEMIES ACCUSE HIM, FALSELY, OF BRINGING GENTILES INTO GOD'S HOUSE WHERE ONLY JEWS ARE ALLOWED.

THERE HE IS -- THE TRAITOR!

HE HAS DEFILED THIS HOLY PLACE OF GOD!

IN ANGER THE PEOPLE TURN AGAINST PAUL. A MOB DRAGS HIM FROM THE TEMPLE AND STARTS TO BEAT HIM.

LOOK OUT-- ROMAN SOLDIERS ARE COMING!

NOW, TELL US WHAT THIS MAN HAS DONE.

TAKE HIM AWAY-- KILL HIM!

THE SOLDIERS CARRY PAUL TO THE PRISON. ON ITS STEPS PAUL STOPS AND TELLS THE PEOPLE HOW HE BECAME A CHRISTIAN, BUT WHEN HE MENTIONS PREACHING TO THE GENTILES, THE MOB GOES WILD.

HE IS NOT FIT TO LIVE!

KILL HIM!

KILL HIM!

TO PROTECT PAUL'S LIFE, THE ROMAN COMMANDER AT JERUSALEM SENDS HIM TO CAESAREA, WHERE PAUL IS KEPT IN PRISON. AFTER TWO YEARS PAUL APPEARS BEFORE FESTUS, THE ROMAN GOVERNOR, AND DEMANDS HIS RIGHT TO BE TRIED BY THE EMPEROR NERO AT ROME. BUT FIRST FESTUS BRINGS PAUL BEFORE A NEIGHBORING RULER, KING AGRIPPA, WHO IS VISITING THE CITY.

I ONCE THOUGHT IT MY DUTY TO OPPOSE JESUS. I HAD MANY OF HIS FOLLOWERS IMPRISONED. BUT ON MY WAY TO DAMASCUS I SAW A LIGHT FROM HEAVEN... AND JESUS SAID TO ME, "I SEND YOU TO TURN PEOPLE OF ALL NATIONS FROM THE POWER OF SATAN TO GOD... O KING AGRIPPA, I COULD NOT DISOBEY THE HEAVENLY VISION.

YOU'RE TRYING TO PERSUADE ME TO BE A CHRISTIAN.

216

FESTUS AND AGRIPPA WOULD HAVE SET PAUL FREE IF HE HAD NOT DEMANDED A TRIAL IN ROME. SO--UNDER ROMAN GUARD AND ACCOMPANIED BY LUKE-- PAUL IS TAKEN ABOARD A SHIP BOUND FOR ROME. AT THE ISLAND OF CRETE...

THE WINTER STORMS WILL SOON BE HERE. IT WILL BE DANGEROUS TO GO ON UNTIL SPRING.

THE HARBOR AT PHOENIX IS NOT FAR AWAY--WE'LL SPEND THE WINTER THERE.

THE SHIP SETS SAIL--ONLY TO BE STRUCK BY A RAGING "NORTHEASTER."

TAKE DOWN THE MAINSAIL!

ON THE 14TH NIGHT OF THE STORM THE SAILORS TRY TO DESERT THE SHIP.

UNLESS THOSE MEN STAY WITH THE SHIP, YOU CANNOT BE SAVED!

THE SOLDIERS CUT THE SMALL BOAT LOOSE --AND THE SAILORS ARE FORCED TO STAY WITH THE SHIP. AT DAYBREAK...

LAND AHEAD!

HEADING TOWARD A BAY, THE SHIP RUNS AGROUND. THE BOW STICKS FAST, BUT THE STERN BEGINS TO BREAK UNDER THE POUNDING OF THE HEAVY WAVES.

ABANDON SHIP!

KILL THE PRISONERS--IF THEY REACH SHORE THEY'LL ESCAPE.

BECAUSE OF HIS FRIENDSHIP FOR PAUL, THE ROMAN OFFICER SPARES THE PRISONERS. SOLDIERS, SAILORS, PASSENGERS, AND PRISONERS STRUGGLE FOR THEIR LIVES IN THE RAGING SEA.

The people watch to see if Paul will swell up or fall over dead. When nothing happens, the islanders change their minds and say that Paul must have God-given powers.

Life in Bible Times

It's easy to take some of our modern-day conveniences for granted, isn't it? Have you ever wondered what it would have been like to live when Jesus did? If you wanted a drink, a trip to the local well was in order.

In this section, you'll see what life was like two thousand years ago in Palestine.

When it's time for bed and the fire has died down to a few glowing coals, a board will be laid over it and then a carpet. This keeps the room warm for hours. The family sleeps on mattresses spread on the floor.

AT HOME IN PALESTINE

The lower floor of the average house was used as a stable for animals when they couldn't be left outdoors. At other times it served as a workshop or a playroom.

MOST HOMES IN PALESTINE HAD TWO FLOORS. THE PEOPLE USED THEIR FLAT ROOFS FOR MANY ACTIVITIES, BUT THE SECOND FLOOR WAS THEIR MAIN LIVING QUARTERS. HERE THEY SLEPT AT NIGHT, DID THEIR COOKING AND STORED THEIR BELONGINGS. THIS PICTURE WE SEE A TYPICAL FAMILY IN THE SECOND FLOOR OF THEIR HOME.

FATHER IS BRINGING HOME A SACK OF WHEAT. THE GIRL AND BOY ARE GRINDING FLOUR. MOTHER IS TAKING SOMETHING OUT OF ONE OF THE "CLOSETS" (THEIR CLOSETS WERE JUST "PIGEON HOLES" IN THE MUD WALLS). THE FIRE IS A LARGE HOLE IN THE FLOOR, FILLED WITH BURNING CHARCOAL.

ONE THING TO BE SAID IN FAVOR OF THE CLOTHING STYLES IN JESUS' TIME IS THAT THEY DIDN'T CHANGE FROM YEAR TO YEAR AS OURS DO TODAY. PEOPLE NOW LIVING IN THAT PART OF THE WORLD DRESS JUST ABOUT THE SAME AS THEY DID, 1959 YEARS AGO... AND AS THEY HAD FOR HUNDREDS OF YEARS BEFORE JESUS WAS BORN.

LABORERS USUALLY WORE ONLY THE UNDERGARMENT—WITH OR WITHOUT SLEEVES—OR MERELY A WAIST-CLOTH WHICH REACHED TO THEIR KNEES.

A WIDE GIRDLE AROUND THEIR WAIST SERVED AS "POCKETS" IN WHICH THEY CARRIED MONEY, FOOD, A SWORD OR DAGGER, ETC.

"FAMILY FASHIONS in the FIRST CENTURY

SOME WORE A PLAIN SHEET WOUND AROUND THE BODY WITH ONE END FLUNG OVER THE SHOULDER. JESUS IS USUALLY PICTURED DRESSED THAT WAY.

GIRLS WORE THE SAME KIND OF CLOTHING AS THEIR MOTHERS WORE... WHICH, BY THE WAY, WAS PRACTICALLY THE SAME AS THE MEN WORE. IN FACT, SOME OF THE GARMENTS WERE SO MUCH ALIKE THAT THEY COULD BE WORN BY EITHER MEN OR WOMEN, AND NO ONE WOULD KNOW THE DIFFERENCE, EXCEPT FOR THE HEADDRESS. WOMEN AND GIRLS WORE LONG HEAD SCARFS.

OCCUPATIONS IN BIBLE TIMES

FARMERS IN JESUS' TIME DIDN'T LIVE ON THEIR FARMS. THEY LIVED IN THE VILLAGES FOR MUTUAL PROTECTION FROM WILD ANIMALS AND BANDITS. EACH MORNING THE FARMERS WOULD DRIVE THEIR ANIMALS TO THEIR FIELDS FOR THE DAY'S WORK, WHICH BEGAN AT SUNRISE AND ENDED AT SUNSET.

MOST OF THE SMALL FARMS IN PALESTINE WERE WORKED BY THE FARMER'S FAMILY. BUT MANY MEN WHO DID NOT OWN FARMS WOULD HIRE THEMSELVES OUT AS FARM WORKERS.

A SHEPHERD'S LIFE IN BIBLE TIMES WAS FILLED WITH DANGER AND HARDSHIP. HE WAS ON GUARD DAY AND NIGHT PROTECTING HIS SHEEP FROM RUSTLERS AND WILD ANIMALS. HIS DEFENSES AGAINST THESE LURKING DANGERS WERE HIS STAFF, HIS SLING AND HIS COURAGE.

SHEPHERDS USED A SLING WITH AMAZING ACCURACY. THE SMALL STONES THEY HURLED STRUCK WITH TERRIFIC FORCE. DAVID SLEW THE GIANT GOLIATH WITH A SHEPHERD'S SLING. (1 SAMUEL 17:32–51)

THE SLING WAS A SHORT STRIP OF LEATHER. A WIDE PIECE IN THE CENTER HELD THE SMALL STONE. AFTER WHIRLING THE SLING AROUND HIS HEAD A FEW TIMES, THE SHEPHERD LET GO OF ONE END, SENDING THE STONE SPEEDING LIKE A BULLET TOWARD THE TARGET.

AT NIGHT FLOCKS WERE BROUGHT INTO A SHEEPFOLD FOR PROTECTION. AS EACH SHEEP ENTERED, IT WAS COUNTED—EVEN CALLED BY NAME. THROUGHOUT THE NIGHT THE SHEPHERD SLEPT AT THE OPENING OF THE FOLD, ACTING AS THE VERY GATE ITSELF.

LIFE IN BIBLE TIMES WAS QUITE DIFFERENT FROM TODAY. BUT THE WORDS JESUS PREACHED IN THE NEW TESTAMENT APPLY TO US AS MUCH AS THEY DID TO THESE PEOPLE WHO LIVED 2,000 YEARS AGO.

223

IF YOU LIKED
THESE GREAT ADVENTURES,
YOU'LL LOVE
OWNING THE ENTIRE BIBLE
IN PICTURE STRIPS!

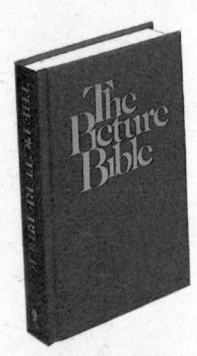

The Picture Bible

Here is the complete Bible—in full-color picture strips. The **Picture Bible** combines beautiful, well-researched art with an easy-to-understand text. It makes the Bible come alive! Join the millions who've read and loved this best-selling format. All 750 pages are in full color. For ages 9 and up. Available in hardcover or paperback.

The Living Picture Bible

Your children will love reading their very own Bible. The **Living Picture Bible** combines the entire New Testament of the best-selling Living Bible with hundreds of fascinating full-color illustrations. A great Bible for kids! It contains introductions to each book, historical maps and notes, large print, and a strong binding. You'll find your kids reading it again and again—just for fun! 709 pages. Hardcover.